REVELATION: HOPE IN THE DARKNESS

Scotty Smith

STUDY GUIDE WITH LEADER'S NOTES

New
Growth
Press
newgrowthpress.com

New Growth Press, Greensboro, NC 27404
newgrowthpress.com
Copyright © 2020 by Scotty Smith

Unless otherwise indicated, Scripture quotations are taken from The
Holy Bible, New International Version®, NIV®. Copyright © 1973, 1978,
1984, 2011 by Biblica, Inc.® Used by permission. All rights reserved
worldwide.

Scripture quotations labeled (NKJV) are taken from the New
King James Version®. Copyright © 1982 by Thomas Nelson. Used by
permission. All rights reserved.

Cover Design: Faceout Books, faceoutstudio.com
Interior Design and Typesetting: Gretchen Logterman
Exercises and Application Questions: Jack Klumpenhower

ISBN 978-1-64507-072-6 (Print)
ISBN 978-1-64507-090-0 (eBook)

Printed in India

28 27 26 25 24 23 22 21   2 3 4 5 6

CONTENTS

Text: Revelation 1

Article: *The Foundation of All Hope*

Exercise: *False Images of Jesus*

Text: Revelation 2

Article: *Jesus and His Bride*

Exercise: *Burdensome Holiness vs. Beautiful Holiness*

Text: Revelation 3

Article: *True Life, Joy, and Riches*

Exercise: *The Beautiful Bride and the Loving Savior*

Text: Revelation 4

Article: *An Occupied Throne*

Exercise: *God Reigns*

Text: Revelation 5

Article: *The Perfected Worship of Heaven*

Exercise: *Approaches to Worship*

Text: Revelation 6–7

Article: *The Last Days*

Exercise: *Using the Bible to Reflect on Suffering*

Text: Revelation 8–10

Article: *Justice Is Coming*

Exercise: *The Bittersweet Gospel*

INTRODUCTION

The book of Revelation has suffered at the hands of its many interpreters though the years. Many simply want to treat the last book of the Bible as though it were a prophetic jigsaw puzzle, written to be solved for the final generation of Christians. Others dismiss it as being too veiled, complex, and culture-bound to be of any benefit to modern believers. Some so spiritualize the text as to render it little more than a book of parables and allegories.

In the early years of my life in Christ, I was exposed to a certain very detailed analysis of Revelation—and all the charts that came with it—which was presented as the one and only correct handling of the text. This particular school of interpretation led me and many of my young Christian friends to develop some wrong thinking and habits. I found myself spending too much time listening to the latest news reports in order to interpret biblical prophecy (I am still trying to find those Viet Cong helicopters in the text!). I was too taken up with end-times sensationalism.

I was also influenced to be far more preoccupied with Satan and the pervasiveness of evil than I was aware of our sovereign God, ruling over all things from his throne in heaven, and of the triumphant Lamb of God who came "to destroy the devil's work" (1 John 3:8). This led me to withdraw from my culture out of fear, into the false "safety" of an ingrown Christian subculture.

Lastly, the teaching I received on Revelation prompted me to develop an individualized spirituality. I had little understanding of the importance of the church and our corporate life as the people of God. Much of this was driven by fear and an inadequate view of the gospel. I remember receiving a lot of emphasis on being an overcomer through discipline and trying harder to please God. I

1

wasn't taught to trust boldly in Jesus and in his all-sufficient grace. Since I am a proud man who loves to perform, I became a Pharisee among Pharisees. Today, I'm a Pharisee in recovery.

I finally came to the point of giving up on the book of Revelation. It became a closed part of the Scripture to me for several years. It wasn't until I was prevailed upon for months (hounded is more like it!) to offer a study of the book of Revelation that I dared to venture back into this part of God's Word associated with so many bad memories.

However, an unbiased study of the text, along with good resourcing and research, led me literally to *see* Revelation in a whole new light. What a surprise our heavenly Father had in store for me as I sought to read and ponder it as though I were a part of the first community of faith in Asia Minor to receive John's series of visions! I have never enjoyed examining and teaching a portion of the Bible more than the year we spent working through this text. It was wonderful to rejoice with childlike wonder at what God was opening to us through his Scriptures.

These studies are the fruit of that discovery. I will share with you what we found to be both true and freeing.

Let me say at the outset that I offer nothing new or novel. No angel has appeared to me to reveal secrets others have missed. I make no claim to original thoughts or exegesis. Everything you will read in this study has been said before and with more precision. If that were not the case, I would be both crazy and presumptuous! My joy is simply to creatively restate these things for God's people of my generation.

I am also driven by a heartfelt concern for the hurting and biblically hungry people of God, and by their pronounced need for hope—a real, substantive hope. The older I have gotten as a Christian, husband, dad, son, friend, and pastor, the more I am constrained to conclude that life is hard, very hard. My own formula-based spirituality of the late '60s and '70s, with its principles and promises for "abundant living," has faded into a more honest, if painful, understanding of the normal Christian life.

The theologically thin veneer of name-it-and-claim-it prosperity teaching (by which I was also influenced for a season) has been exposed for what it really is: a vain attempt to tame and control the sovereign purposes of Almighty God.

This is where God's good gift of hope comes in. In the Scriptures, hope is a present state of confidence based on the guarantee of a glorious future. To hope is to become so familiar with the future of God's story that it invades our daily lives now. By faith, we begin to smell the grass of the new heaven and new earth. The incomparable wonders of what is ahead for God's people are brought to bear upon our present, difficult circumstances, and mission opportunities. When our Lord returns, he will make all things new, beautiful, and right!

Such confidence frees Christians in every age and place to rejoice despite suffering and even to embrace suffering in the form of sacrificial love for God and others. "In this you greatly rejoice, though now for a little while you may have had to suffer grief in all kinds of trials" (1 Peter 1:6). Hope does not replace grief and trials; it wondrously transforms them.

I am convinced beyond all doubt that the last book in the Bible was written primarily to stimulate the people of God in every generation to *great hope*. This makes Revelation greatly accessible, deeply encouraging, and highly practical for how each of us lives today.

This book of overwhelming sights, nearly-audible sounds, and rich symbols is not just meant to bring eternal encouragement and liberating perspective in the final days before the coming of Jesus, nor is it just for the first-century church seeking to deal with the violent persecution of the Roman world. Rather, I have come to rejoice in the present hope offered to Christians of every generation by this timely and timeless book. Followers of the Lamb everywhere, and in all periods of church history, face struggles, fears, and heartaches similar to those of the first readers of Revelation. The setting and the circumstances vary, but spiritual warfare goes on wherever the people of God live. It is to the whole people of God that this book of hope is sent.

HOW TO USE THIS STUDY

This study guide will help you study Revelation within a group. Studying with other believers in Christ lets you benefit from what God is also teaching them, and it gives you encouragement and accountability as you apply what you learn.

Like the other resources in this series, this study is gospel-centered. This means the study begins with an assumption that you have a daily need for the gospel. You have fears and insecurities and sins that the saving work of Jesus addresses, and by looking to the gospel you grow in love for Jesus and, in turn, a desire to love others and take the gospel out to them. With this in mind, the group will be a place to be open about sins and struggles with the goal of growing in Christ, gaining confidence as you see how he saves you in every way from that sin.

Each participant should have one of these study guides in order to join in reading and be able to work through the exercises during that part of the study. *The study leader should read through both the lesson and the leader's notes in the back of this book before each lesson begins.* Because Revelation is a lengthy book of the Bible, two lessons (lessons 7 and 11) require each participant to read a few chapters from Revelation on their own before arriving for the study. Otherwise, no preparation or homework is required.

There are fourteen lessons in this study guide. Each lesson will take about an hour to complete, perhaps a bit more if your group is large, and will include these elements:

BIG IDEA. This is a summary of the main point of the lesson.

BIBLE CONVERSATION. You will read a chapter or two from Revelation and discuss that passage. As the heading suggests, the

Bible conversation questions are intended to spark a conversation rather than generate correct answers. In most cases, the questions will have several possible good answers and a few best answers. The leader's notes at the back of this book provide some insights, but don't just turn there for the "right answer." At times you may want to see what the notes say, but always try to answer for yourself first by thinking about the Bible passage.

ARTICLE. This is the main teaching section of the lesson, written by the book's author.

DISCUSSION. The discussion questions following the article will help you apply the teaching to your life. Again, there will be several good ways to answer each question.

EXERCISE. The exercise is a section you will complete on your own during group time. You can write in the book if that helps you. You will then share some of what you learned with the group. If the group is large, it may help to split up to share the results of the exercise and to pray, so that everyone has a better opportunity to participate.

WRAP-UP AND PRAYER. Prayer is a critical part of the lesson because your spiritual growth will happen through God's work in you, not by your self-effort. You will be asking him to do that good work.

This study guide is based on the author's contributions to the book, *Unveiled Hope: Eternal Encouragement from the Book of Revelation*, which the author wrote with Michael Card and first published in 1997. The articles, appendix, and the author's introduction and closing notes in this study guide consist mostly of condensed excerpts from that book. The discussions, exercises, and leader's notes all draw on that book as well. For further study, you may want to consult that entire work. It is available for purchase as an ebook at the New Growth Press website.

1

A VISION OF JESUS

BIG IDEA

Our vision of Jesus tends to be too small. Revelation's purpose is not to give us a puzzle to figure out about Jesus, but to help us clarify and enlarge our vision of him in scary times.

BIBLE CONVERSATION *15 minutes*

In Revelation, seeing the point matters more than solving the puzzle. The book calls itself "the *revelation* of Jesus Christ." The Greek word is *apokalypsis*, which means "unveiling" and refers to a fascinating type of literature. Apocalyptic writing in the Bible uses fanciful imagery to reveal to us what's really happening as we struggle in a world that seems trapped in evil's grip. Things are not simply as they appear to the naked eye. There is a bigger story in play, God's story of redemption and restoration. We are invited to engage our imagination, and our wonder at great spectacle, and see that God is at war with the devil and is certain to win this epic clash. So, God is using these vivid pictures to show us, in symbols, the deeper reality of how he is redeeming and restoring his world. He wants to arouse in us a child-like awe and confidence in our Savior.

Chapter 1 sets this up as a revelation from Jesus to the apostle John, who is on the island of Patmos in the Aegean Sea and in turn shares the revelation with seven churches on the nearby main-land of Asia Minor, modern-day Turkey. Fittingly, it begins with a vision of Jesus himself. This is easily the most detailed physical description of Jesus found anywhere in the Bible. But of course, the point is not to show us what Jesus actually looks like physically. The meaning behind the description is where the true glory lies.

Have someone read **Revelation 1** aloud, or have several readers take turns. Then discuss the questions below:

Verse 3 says it will be a blessing for you to read and take to heart the words of Revelation. Think of what you just read. What part struck you as particularly helpful already, and why?

Revelation is thought of as a book about the future, but what do you find most encouraging about the things chapter 1 says Jesus has already done for us in the past? What's encouraging about who he is for us today, in the present?

Think about John's response to the vision of Jesus starting in verse 17, and Jesus's response to John. How closely does it resemble your relationship with Jesus, and how would you like your relationship with Jesus to become more like it?

****

Now read the following article, written by this book's author. Take turns reading it aloud, switching readers at each paragraph break. Then discuss the questions at the end of the article.

THE FOUNDATION OF ALL HOPE

5 MINUTES

One of the scariest moments of my life occurred when I was about six years old. Our family was vacationing on the Potomac River. One afternoon, as we decided to cross the big river in a small wooden ski boat, the sky suddenly became blacker than any I have seen before or since. The placid waters upon which I had learned to water ski that week became pitching waves, big enough to surf. What took my fears to an all-time high were the words spoken by the captain of our overcrowded and undersized craft: "We have little gas and no anchor." The thought of being anchorless, adrift and helpless, caused raw terror.

It was on such a turbulent "sea" of confusion, fear, and uncertainty that the book of Revelation was written. John, the aged apostle, is in an involuntary exile on Patmos "because of the word of God and the testimony of Jesus." Meanwhile on the mainland, the people of God are involved in a deadly conflict with the world. Intense spiritual warfare is escalating. Persecution is no longer occasional and local, but regular and widespread. And within the church's gates, heresy, immorality, and worldliness are growing as the second century prepares to dawn.

At such a time, and to such a people, John writes of a Sovereign Lord and a Savior Lamb. There is no trace of panic, fear, or defeatism. Instead, there is encouragement, insight, worship, and hope! What do those believers, and we today, most need at this time and in every season of life? We need to see Jesus! He is our anchor! Until Jesus returns, life won't be without its storms, but we'll never experience a Christ-absent day.

To see Jesus is to have hope. His complete triumph over sin and all evil is the dominant theme of Revelation. Jesus is set forth as everything we need in life and in death, in prosperity and in adversity, in joy and in tribulation. John is making the point that the main question in life is "How big and how good is your Jesus?"

Consider what God wants us to know about our Savior in chapter 1 alone: Jesus is the "faithful witness." We can trust him without hesitation, for he is the Word of God, truth incarnate. Jesus is "the ruler of the kings of the earth"—right now, not in the distant future. We can be sure that our God reigns and has no rivals. And Jesus is "the firstborn from the dead" who "has freed us from our sins by his blood." His resurrection guarantees ours. His shed blood secured our forever freedom. What greater comfort can be found than to know that the Lord of the universe has set his affection on us—even us! Jesus is the prophet, priest, and king we always wanted, and always needed—the Yes to every promise God has made.

As John ponders such love, he cannot help but think of the time when this outpouring of grace will be perfected in us. He who loves us is coming back for us! "Look, he is coming with the clouds, and 'every eye will see him.'" For those who have received his grace, which flows so freely from the cross, there will be joy unspeakable: our sins, which kept Jesus on his tree of death even more than the nails did, have been forgiven, all of them!

It is important and comforting to notice that the first thing John sees is Jesus in the midst of his people, the church, represented by the seven golden lampstands. Jesus is with us and he is for us. John goes on to describe Jesus in rich imagery and symbolism that is not meant to be painted, but rather to be pondered—scripturally. Two-thirds of the verses in Revelation contain at least one allusion to an Old Testament passage. The only "code language" John is using is that of God's Word.

- The "son of man" in John's vision is none other than the glorious persona described by the same name in Daniel 7:13. This is the title Jesus chose when referring to himself during his ministry. Deliverance from the Babylonian captivity was just a foreshadowing of the deliverance from sin that Jesus would win for us in fulfilling Daniel's prophecies.

- John sees Jesus clothed with a robe, perhaps representative of both a king and a high priest. Jesus is the King of kings and the Lord of lords, and he is the faithful and merciful high priest presiding over a throne of grace for the people of God! The golden sash speaks of his authority (see Exodus 28:8).

- The white hair is an expression of wisdom and the respect due him. This is none other than Daniel's "Ancient of Days" (Daniel 7:9).

- The penetrating scrutiny of our Lord is symbolized by his eyes "like blazing fire." His stability and strength are emphasized by his feet "like bronze glowing in a furnace." John describes the voice he hears as having the might and authority of "rushing waters," the very expression Ezekiel 1:24 uses to describe the voice of God.

- In Jesus's right hand are the seven stars which represent the angels, or messengers, of the seven churches. Once again, we have a picture of the involvement and care our Lord gives to his people.

- The "doubled-edged sword" that issues from his mouth shows that his words are true and powerful. He speaks grace for his people and destruction for his enemies (see Isaiah 11:4).

- Lastly, the face of Jesus is seen in all of its overwhelming brilliance. "Like the sun," his glory shines forth (see Malachi 4:2).

The hand of grace touches John as these great words of encouragement are spoken: "Do not be afraid"—the most repeated command in the Bible. That is all we need to hear from Jesus. History is moving inexorably toward God's determined end. There are no contingency plans in heaven, no mere probabilities; no vexation, consternation, or Plan B. Everything is assured. This is neither fate nor karma. This is King Jesus. All we need is to see him, the biblical Jesus, the real Jesus. He is our anchor of hope, ocean of grace, and final destination.

DISCUSSION *10 MINUTES*

What troubles in the world today, or in your life, make you feel scared or defeated? What difference does it make to see that Jesus loves to encourage his people with the assurance that he is overcoming these troubles?

Think about the meanings behind the description of Jesus. Which aspect of him do you sometimes tend to overlook? How would it help you to notice that truth about Jesus more often?

1

EXERCISE

FALSE IMAGES OF JESUS

20 MINUTES

All of us have been exposed to images of Jesus, either actual pictures or images in our minds, that fall short of the imagery presented in Revelation 1. Having a right view of Jesus begins with exposing these false images.

For this exercise, begin by working on your own. Read through the exercise and consider your responses, writing them down if that helps. When the group is ready, you'll have an opportunity to share some of your results.

Step 1. Think about some false images of Jesus. Be honest: which of them reflect the way you sometimes think about Jesus, even if you know better? Or which views do you encounter when you talk to others about Jesus?

❏ Shampoo-Advertisement Jesus
Clean and fresh, with sheen in his wavy hair. A good model. Inspires people to try to look their best, be their best, and feel their best.

❏ Coloring-Page Jesus
Flat and lifeless. Despite the familiar stories, has never come off the page and felt alive.

❐ Family-Movie Jesus

Nice guy with kind eyes. One-dimensional. Glides through the world spouting parables and using trance-like hand gestures to heal people while the crowd parts before him so his linen robes won't get wrinkled. Somehow above-the-fray. The last guy in the scene you'd expect to start swinging a sword.

❐ Vending-Machine Jesus

Put in enough payment, press the right buttons, and he might give you what you want. The buyer is in control, and what you can get matters more than the Giver.

❐ Store-at-the-Mall Jesus

One enticing option among many. A good choice for you if he fits your style.

❐ Motivational-Speaker Jesus

Presents easy tips for a successful life. Bids you follow him into comfort and hassle-free living, not sacrifice or repentance.

❐ Church-Statue Jesus

Old, dusty, and institutional. A relic from a bygone era. Interesting to look back on, but not very relevant when it comes to daily life in our times.

❐ Darth Vader Jesus

Represents the evil empire of "organized religion." Potentially damaging. Once a good guy, maybe, but now a symbol of repressive attitudes and hurtful influence.

❐ Santa Claus Jesus

Supposedly a good guy, but always checking up on who's been naughty or nice. Inclined to withhold his gifts if he sees how naughty you've been. Comes around now and then but mostly stays distant, not actually helping you become nicer.

❐ Disguised-as-Moses Jesus
More often seen carrying stone tablets of law than a cross of redemptive love.

❐ Clay-Figure Jesus
Moldable. Always fits who you think he should be. Repeatedly shaped into any viewpoint or political cause you like. Never shapes you.

❐ Other: _____

Step 2. Consider how the imagery in Revelation 1 is a good correction to these false images. What true imagery of Jesus is especially important to notice so we can combat our false images?

I wish people I know would see that Jesus is _____

_____.

I personally need to see that Jesus is _____

_____.

When the group is ready, share some of your responses. What richer view of Jesus is big enough to support you in both world-shaking times and world-changing tasks?

WRAP-UP AND PRAYER *10 MINUTES*

Truth is a gift from God. As part of your prayer time together, ask that the Holy Spirit guide you as you study and help you to see the true Jesus clearly, and to worship him as John did.

2

JESUS'S LOVE FOR HIS CHURCH

BIG IDEA

Jesus has passionate love for his bride, the church, and so he both encourages her and rebukes her.

BIBLE CONVERSATION *20 MINUTES*

Having shown who he is and how he's among his people, Jesus now reveals his message for his churches. He chooses seven churches not far from Patmos to receive letters, but they are representative of all of his people. As an involved Lover of his people, Jesus's love often gets painful. His letters include both life-powering encouragements and life-preserving rebukes (he will say to one of the churches later, in chapter 3, "Those whom I love I rebuke and discipline").

Have a few readers take turns reading aloud through **Revelation 2**, which contains the first four letters. Then discuss the questions below.

What do you appreciate about the approach and tone Jesus takes in his letters? Give some examples.

Each letter starts with a description of Jesus and ends with a promise for those who remain faithful. Which descriptions or promises do you find especially motivating, and why?

Why might it be important to start and end a letter of commendation and rebuke with reminders of the person and promises of Jesus?

Externally, the church in Smyrna appears to be doing the worst: it is suffering much persecution and poverty. Yet it is the only church in this chapter not to receive any rebuke. What might this suggest about the Christian life, or about how Jesus sees his people?

****

Now take turns reading the article aloud, switching readers at each paragraph break. At the end of the article, discuss the questions that follow it.

Lesson

ARTICLE

2

JESUS AND HIS BRIDE

5 MINUTES

Every verse in Revelation resonates with Jesus's love. Our Lord is preparing a bride to marry and love forever. To miss this central theme in Revelation would be a great injustice to the whole book and would deny our hearts profound joy, peace, and comfort. There is no people more loved, right now, than the church of Jesus Christ!

Astonishment and profound gratitude should follow as these truths grip our hearts. As we ponder our future as the people of God, what should thrill us most is not simply leaving this world, with all of its evil and brokenness, but the living hope of the coming wedding supper of the Lamb. And the anticipation and excitement of every groom must certainly fill the heart of Jesus too. Dare we believe that he is looking forward to his second coming even more than we are?

As a pastor I have had the privilege of officiating at many weddings, but one in particular stands out to me. We were at the anxiously awaited, sweaty-palms moment in the service when the bride was to enter. Majestic strains of "Joyful, Joyful, We Adore Thee" filled the sanctuary. The doors to the back of the worship center were pulled opened, and there she was—the bride, as ready and as beautiful as any I have ever seen (except for my wife, of course!).

None of us were prepared for what happened next. All of a sudden, the groom let out a spontaneous "Wow!" and took off up the aisle to receive his bride! He was overwhelmed by the impact of the moment. I had to go after him and physically pull him back into place. Needless to say, we were all deeply touched by the demonstration of his unabated love for his beloved.

What stirs me even more is to realize this is the way Jesus loves us! Anticipation fills his heart as he awaits the opening of the doors of heaven, that he might receive his bride. Jesus is looking forward to his second coming more than we are. The more I read, study, and reflect on Revelation, the more I realize I am just beginning to perceive the infectious, intense, and involved love of Jesus for his church. Let's take a look now at what Jesus commends and what he corrects in these churches he loves.

THE CHURCH IN EPHESUS

Decades earlier, the apostle Paul had concluded his Ephesian epistle with this benediction: "Grace to all who love our Lord Jesus Christ with an undying love." Sadly, undying love gave way to forsaken love in Ephesus. Here is a church commended for her hard work, perseverance, and defense of the faith in the face of heresy. And yet, here is a church that has lost the heart of a bride. She is Martha, so busy *for* Jesus, rather than Mary who treasured communion *with* Jesus more than anything else.

The correction Jesus brings is as much a compliment as it is a rebuke. Do we realize what it means for our Lord to be jealous for our love? He who loves us with an everlasting love is calling for affection and pronounced love from us, his bride. What dignity! What delight!

THE CHURCH IN SMYRNA

As I read Jesus's letter to Smyrna, I am struck by his tenderness, compassion, and involved love. To the bride who is suffering he reveals himself as "the First and the Last, who died and came to life again." He is victorious! We need not fear death, even death by martyrdom.

I am also deeply encouraged by the fact that Jesus both acknowledges our suffering and reveals himself to be the Lord over our pain. He who has been made perfect through his own suffering knows our limits, even as he also knows his purposes for our sufferings. How freeing it is to know that pain and faithfulness go hand in hand. Suffering is not a sign that we lack faith, but a sign of the depth of our love. Let us pray that God will enable us to rejoice in our sufferings and to see in the sufferings of our Lord not just the payment for our freedom but also the pattern for our lifestyle.

THE CHURCH IN PERGAMUM

Pergamum was a center for philosophy and religion, so it is not hard to understand why this was a persecuted church. To be a Christian is to commit to a monogamous relationship with the Lover of our souls. This truth is offensive to a world which champions many ways to the same god. The cost of living out a compassionate demonstration and defense of the truth of the gospel can be great. Antipas, a member of the church, lost his life for the sake of truth in Pergamum.

Yet Jesus rebukes his bride for being inconsistent in her very strength: love for the truth. Compromise with pagan idolatry and immorality was being introduced to the fellowship, perhaps by those who thought Christians were being a little too exclusive. Jesus reminds us that we must not tolerate error under the guise of being open-minded and fair. The bride in love must also be the bride in truth.

THE CHURCH IN THYATIRA

The one who sees everything, with his eyes of blazing fire, looks into the heart of the church in Thyatira and finds much to affirm. But the challenge of buying and selling in an economy in which business was tied to false worship was taking its toll. Economic pressure led to moral compromise. Perhaps some Christians thought it would be possible to cooperate with certain trade guilds without being influenced by their worldview and lifestyle. They were naïve.

In confronting this evil, Jesus calls his bride to a more consistent and consuming holiness. *Holiness* is one of those words that has fallen on hard times in the contemporary church. Before I became a Christian, this church word sounded synonymous with dourness, the interjection *NO!*, and mean-spirited people who did anything but make the gospel attractive to me. But now, as God has given me grace, I realize that holiness is an attitude of the heart before it is compliance with an external code.

In the context of the bridegroom-bride metaphor, holiness is our radical commitment to live out the implications of what it means to be the tenderly-loved bride of Jesus. We are to live for the pleasure and praise of Jesus, not that he might accept us, but because he already has—fully and eternally! We are to demonstrate to the watching world what it means to be captured by the love of Jesus in the gospel. As a betrothed bride, let us keep ourselves pure and holy for our true love.

DISCUSSION *10 minutes*

What do you tend to imagine is the look in Jesus's eyes when he thinks of you? What difference might it make to realize you are a beautiful bride in the eyes of your Lover?

Loss of life due to faith in Jesus is mentioned several times in this chapter of Revelation. How much have you thought about that possibility for yourself, and is this a weakness or a strength in your Christian life?

Lesson

EXERCISE

2

BURDENSOME HOLINESS VS. BEAUTIFUL HOLINESS

15 MINUTES

Jesus's delight for his holy bride is spelled out in Ephesians 5:25–27. "Christ loved the church and gave himself up for her to make her holy, cleansing her by the washing with water through the word, and to present her to himself as a radiant church, without stain or wrinkle or any other blemish, but holy and blameless."

To be *holy* is simply to be "set apart" for God's good purposes. Even if we know better, sometimes we think wrongly about Jesus's love for us and our holiness, and we miss its beauty.

- We imagine we need to make ourselves holy enough in order to keep Jesus loving us, and so we resent his call to be holy. It feels like a **BURDENSOME HOLINESS**.

- We forget that it is Jesus who makes us holy, and that he does it because he loves us, and so we fail to appreciate that his call to be holy is about a **BEAUTIFUL HOLINESS**.

Working on your own, consider the differences between a **BUR-DENSOME** approach to holiness and a **BEAUTIFUL** one. Pick some differences that are meaningful to you, or that make you eager to be more holy, or that represent ways you want to grow. When the group is ready, you'll share some of your findings.

BURDENSOME "HOLINESS"	BEAUTIFUL HOLINESS
Holiness is my performance for God (and for others who might be watching).	Holiness is God's beauty-making project in me (which I get to join in on). "May God himself, the God of peace, sanctify you through and through" (1 Thessalonians 5:23).
I can dress myself up, but I feel like God knows the truth. I look pretty ugly to him, not at all holy.	Praise God! I know that in the past, at the cross, Jesus died for my sin and God declared me holy. *Holy* is my identity before God—who I really am. "You were washed, you were sanctified" (1 Corinthians 6:11).
I try to work on being holy, but it's hard and I fail all the time. I feel as if Jesus is looking down on me, impatient, and constantly disappointed in what he sees.	Praise God! I know that in the present God is actively working in my life, patiently teaching me to live like the holy person I am. What a privilege! What loving care! "We all . . . are being transformed into his image with ever-increasing glory" (2 Corinthians 3:18).
I want to go to heaven, so I guess I better work on holiness.	Praise God! I know that in the future, when this life is over, God will make my holiness complete. Holiness now is hard, but I work at it because I'm eager to live like a citizen of heaven, bound to feast with Jesus. "When Christ appears, we shall be like him" (1 John 3:2).
Being holy is first of all about measuring up to external rules others will notice and approve of.	Being holy is first of all an attitude of my heart. "Create in me a pure heart, O God" (Psalm 51:10).
I feel a need to define holiness in ways that make it doable on my own, so I end up compromising with morality and worldly idols—and trying to hide those compromises.	Jesus is my captain in my fight for holiness, so I take on all holy-living challenges and dare to expose all kinds of sin in my life. "For the Spirit God gave us does not make us timid, but gives us power, love and self-discipline" (2 Timothy 1:7).

BURDENSOME "HOLINESS"	BEAUTIFUL HOLINESS
My holiness is mostly limited to a <u>physical</u> set-apart-ness. It's about what I may watch, where I may go, whom I may be with, etc.	My holiness goes deeper, becoming a <u>character</u> set-apart-ness. It's about how I love, rejoice, repent, trust God, put myself last, etc. "Set an example for the believers in speech, in conduct, in love, in faith and in purity" (1 Timothy 4:12).
Holy living is chiefly about <u>withdrawing</u> from the culture around me in an attempt to stay pure.	Holy living is chiefly about <u>reaching out</u> to others and sacrificially loving them in an attempt to display the beauty of Jesus. "Now that you have purified yourselves by obeying the truth so that you have sincere love for each other, love one another deeply, from the heart" (1 Peter 1:22).

When the group is ready, share some of the differences that stand out to you. How do you most want to grow in a "beautiful holiness" approach to life with your Savior?

WRAP-UP AND PRAYER *10 minutes*

Part of Jesus's joy over you finds its fulfillment when you pray. God delights for you to turn to him for comfort and help. Pray together for the ways you want him to continue making you into his beautiful bride.

Lesson

3

JESUS'S WORK OF REVIVAL

BIG IDEA

The church is often in danger of becoming complacent and comfortable. We need the repentance and revival our Savior brings.

BIBLE CONVERSATION *20 MINUTES*

Where we left off, Jesus was writing lovingly to his church, using both commendations and rebukes while reminding them of himself and his gospel promises. Have a few readers take turns reading through **Revelation 3** aloud. Then talk about questions below:

Think about the church in Sardis, described as dead and asleep. Based on what you know about how churches lose their aliveness and wakefulness, what was likely going on there?

Now think about the church in Philadelphia, described as having an open door in front of them. Based on what you've seen in churches, why might they still need encouragement to walk through the door God has opened for them?

Finally, think about the church in Laodicea, advised to buy true gold, white clothes, and eye salve. What poor substitutes do you suspect they had bought into in place of treasures in heaven, forgiveness in Christ, and God's truth?

****

Now read the article aloud, taking turns by paragraph, and discuss the questions at the end.

Lesson

ARTICLE

TRUE LIFE, JOY, AND RICHES

5 MINUTES

My friend Michael Card once told me of a visit he had with a couple of national pastors he met while on a mission to China. These men had been imprisoned for nearly twenty years simply because they preached the gospel. He recounted a surprising commitment they had: "to pray about the poverty of the wealth of the American church." Riches and comforts, they feared, were too much of a burden for Christians to carry. "How can Americans be free to love and to worship and to serve Jesus when weighed down with the things of this world?" they lovingly asked. Ouch!

The concern those pastors had about wealth and comfort in churches today might also be applied to the churches in Revelation 3. Here we see both the danger of complacent comfort and the value of hard, humble repentance.

THE CHURCH IN SARDIS

There is no church among the seven which incurs a more severe rebuke from Jesus than Sardis. Here is an example of a bride in name only. She had a reputation without reality, a creed without Christ, religion without relationship. The bride of Jesus is not to be a lifeless mannequin in the window of the religious market-place nor an old, fading image in the scrapbook of ecclesiastical memory. We are called to life—life in the Spirit, generated and sustained by Jesus himself.

Having been a pastor for many years, I realize that the religious and social enculturation in a society can be so strong and deceptive that it is quite possible for large groups of professing Christians to go through the motions of religious life and neither understand the gospel nor experience its saving power. It is one thing to know that you are not a Christian, but quite another to assume that you are joined to Christ when in reality you are only joined to a church. This truth is a part of my own testimony. I assumed I was a Christian up till the night I was converted! We dare not equate being in the pews with being in Christ.

THE CHURCH IN PHILADELPHIA

Jesus reveals himself to the beloved of Philadelphia as the Lord of opportunity. In this church we find a thrilling example of the strength of weakness. This small, seemingly insignificant body of believers is called to go through a great door of opportunity into a life of substantive impact. The gospel is full of such glorious paradoxes: The way to live is to die. The first shall be last. The way up is down. The way to find ourselves is by losing ourselves.

Jesus is calling his humble bride to a life of meaningful ministry and impact. As I read his words here, I am both encouraged and rebuked. I am encouraged that he is the one through whom and by whom all ministry is realized. Jesus uses his people to do things we cannot do in our own power. He calls us, gifts us, and empowers us to be involved in his eternal purposes. He is actively filling up heaven with men and women from every race, tribe, tongue, and people group.

This also rebukes me, and perhaps many of us in the contemporary "fortress church." Believers in Philadelphia were placed in a strategic location at the juncture of trade routes in a pagan culture. All they had to do was walk through the door of opportunity and ministry. Their calling was not to build "camp God" and be a community of navel-gazers merely holding on. Their calling, and ours, is to be salt and light to those who don't yet know Jesus.

The gospel frees us and empowers us to live other-centeredly. Ministry is the costly expression of the love of Jesus. It can get messy, exhausting, and painful. Persecution is the predictable consequence of a commitment to witness faithfully and to love well. But Jesus promises us that he will make those who persecute us "come and fall down at your feet and acknowledge that I have loved you." What an image! What a promise!

THE CHURCH IN LAODICEA

Here we have a picture of an immature and spoiled bride who is blind to her own condition. Jesus confronts his beloved in Laodicea with her spiritual self-satisfaction, complacency, and indifference. Laodicea is an example of a Christian or church that fails to realize how the "good life" can dilute our wholehearted affection for Jesus.

Hear the cry of the Lover of our souls as he calls out to us, "Here I am! I stand at the door and knock. If anyone hears my voice and opens the door, I will come in and eat with that person, and they with me." This is not the appeal of an evangelist to non-Christians. This is Jesus showing us the tragedy of living the Christian life apart from intimacy with him—the evil of having the comforts of this world replace communion with him. He longs to eat with us, to once again enjoy the rich fellowship foreshadowing the greatest fellowship we will ever know, at the wedding supper of the Lamb.

How we, especially in the church in the West today, need to ponder these things! I was present at a lecture in the 1970s where theologian Francis Schaeffer warned us of his fear that we were headed for a day when the consuming preoccupation of American evangelicals would be for personal peace and affluence. God have mercy on us today, decades further down that dangerous road! No matter what our denomination, theological heritage, or liturgical preference, we need revival in the church.

DISCUSSION *10 minutes*

What kinds of concerns might pastors of persecuted churches have for you or for your church? How ready would you be to listen to those concerns?

When it comes to the unbelieving world, is your mentality closer to that of a "fortress church" or that of an advancing church which takes the gospel out? What might it look like for you to live by the article's statement that "the gospel frees us and empowers us to live other-centeredly"?

Lesson

EXERCISE

THE BEAUTIFUL BRIDE AND THE LOVING SAVIOR

15 MINUTES

It seems Jesus chose seven churches—a number meaning fullness, found often in Revelation—for the purpose of giving us a full picture of what the bride of Jesus should look like as she "makes herself ready" for his coming. This full picture allows us to do some assessment.

Work through the exercise on your own. Note what beauty Jesus commends in his church, and how well it fits what you see in the church today, and in yourself. When the group is ready, you'll discuss your responses.

Step 1. Read through the list of features that will be observable in a beautiful bride of Christ based on Jesus's instruction to each church. Note which parts of this picture are true, or not true, of churches in your city—and of you.

A PICTURE OF THE BEAUTIFUL BRIDE

1. EPHESUS – A passionate "first love" relationship with the Lord Jesus which spills over into all other relationships.

2. SMYRNA – A glad willingness and preparedness to suffer for Christ.

3. PERGAMUM – A growing knowledge of the truth of the gospel, and a commitment to defend the faith.

4. THYATIRA – Purity of heart and holiness of lifestyle, driven by love and empowered by grace.

5. SARDIS – An aliveness in Jesus generated by his real presence in our midst and in our hearts.

6. PHILADELPHIA – A commitment to follow Jesus into a life of other-centered living through evangelism, mission, and kingdom impact.

7. LAODICEA – An undivided and wholehearted allegiance to Jesus which treasures communion with him more than the comforts of the world or anything else.

Jesus's people in my city <u>best</u> fit this part of the picture: _____
_____
_____

Jesus's people in my city <u>least</u> fit this part of the picture: _____
_____
_____

By God's grace, I personally <u>best</u> fit the picture in this way: _____
_____
_____

I most need to grow and better fit the picture in this way: _____
_____
_____

Step 2. Remember that each church also is given a description of Jesus, drawn from chapter 1. They (and you!) have help to live like a beautiful bride because the loving Savior is on our side. So now, consider the equally full picture of Jesus given in these letters, and which part most encourages you to live for him.

A PICTURE OF THE LOVING SAVIOR

1. EPHESUS – Your Savior walks among the lampstands. He is with his people!

2. SMYRNA – Your Savior died and came to life again. He has conquered the grave!

3. PERGAMUM – Your Savior has the sharp, double-edged sword. He speaks grace for his people and destruction for their enemies!

4. THYATIRA – Your Savior has eyes like blazing fire and feet like burnished bronze. He sees all and is stronger than all!

5. SARDIS – Your Savior holds the seven spirits of God. He sends his Spirit to comfort and help you!

6. PHILADELPHIA – Your Savior holds the keys. He controls life and death and every opportunity in the world!

7. LAODICEA – Your Savior is the faithful and true witness. You can trust him when the Evil One accuses you!

Believers in my city will be encouraged to live for Jesus when they see that he is: _____

_____

I personally am encouraged to live for Jesus when I see that he is: _____

_____

When the group is ready, share some of your responses. Be sure to talk not only about where you and the church need revival, but also about who Jesus is as the Savior who brings revival.

WRAP-UP AND PRAYER *10 minutes*

One of the best ways we can know we are praying well is to pray for the exact things the Bible tells us Jesus desires for us. As part of your prayer time together, consider praying through the description of the beautiful bride, asking that your loving Savior would make that description true of you.

Lesson

4

JESUS OPENS HEAVEN'S DOOR

BIG IDEA

God is on his throne and rules over all things. We need not fear, nor feel defeated, even in times of real sadness, trouble, and danger.

BIBLE CONVERSATION *20 MINUTES*

Having written personally to his churches, Jesus now gives his people a series of visions that will encourage them in hard times. The first vision is of God's heavenly throne room. Much of the imagery you will encounter as you read about it seems to make the point that God rules over absolutely everything: There is a circular rainbow that doesn't just arch over part of the world but surrounds the whole throne. There is a full number of worshiping elders. There are composite beings representing the vast array of God's creatures—four of them, as if they come from the north, south, east, and west. All of this encircles the throne. God commands it all.

Now have someone read **Revelation 4** aloud. Then discuss the questions below:

Visually, how might you summarize what is seen in God's heavenly throne room? How is it different from popular pictures of heaven in your culture?

What do people end up thinking about God due to popular pictures of heaven? In what better ways *should* we think of God, and of our future with him, based on the imagery in this description?

Now discuss the sounds of heaven presented in this passage. How are they different from the sounds of heaven suggested by popular culture, and how should the auditory symbols in Revelation affect how we think about God and our future with him?

Look at the words used in the worship of God in verse 8 and in verse 11. How do the words fit, and explain, the things seen and heard? Think of several ways they are connected.

＊＊＊＊

Now take turns reading aloud the following article.

Lesson

ARTICLE

AN OCCUPIED THRONE

5 MINUTES

John's readers thought in terms of kings and crowns and thrones. These royal tokens represented life, or sometimes death, to citizens in the Roman world. Christians first tasted the political insanity of Emperor Nero as he sought to blame them for the burning of Rome. And as John writes from Patmos, Emperor Domitian is on the throne and demanding to be addressed as "lord and god." Under his reign, those who call Jesus Lord and God are being severely persecuted and put to death. The Roman throne was a source of fear and anxiety.

Against this backdrop, our Lord who loves to reveal himself opens a door into heaven. John is promised insight into "what must take place after this." Here is that awesome word, *must*. God's will *is* going to be accomplished on earth, even as it is in heaven!

Amid this vision of heaven with all of its glorious persona and perfections, and with all of the sights and sounds and symbols and images and beings, what captures John's attention is a throne with someone sitting on it. An *occupied* throne! It is our heavenly Father! Our God reigns! The *real* throne is in heaven, not in Rome. God rules, not Domitian! All of the kings of the earth are exposed to be frauds like the Wizard of Oz—little men who make a lot of noise behind big curtains.

What makes this throne magnificent is the one who occupies this seat of sovereignty, and his central place in the whole of eternity and time. John does not attempt to tell us what God looks like for fear of even the slightest misrepresentation. All he can say is that he "had the appearance of jasper and ruby." These two precious stones probably are meant to represent God's brilliance and majesty. Our God is altogether glorious.

John also describes "what looked like a sea of glass, clear as crystal." This immense and serene body of water before our enthroned Father conveys the absence of panic in heaven. There are no troubled waters in the dwelling place of God, no consternation or doubt. God is never surprised. He never has anxious moments, nor is he our glorified cheerleader, merely rooting and pulling for us in the game of life. He is God. And he is *our* God, working in all things for the good of those who love him.

How desperately our generation of Christians needs a fresh vision and understanding of the sovereignty of God. We must not be fatalists who sing, "Que sera, sera, whatever will be, will be." Neither may we be stoics, who accept the storms of life with passive resignation. Nor should we become superficial evangelicals, full of denial about the reality of pain and suffering, groping for one more biblical Band-Aid and spiritual anesthetic to deal with huge and troubling issues which are an inevitable part of the Christian life.

Without this vision of the occupied throne, many believers come to the symbols and images in Revelation (like the Antichrist, tribulation, beasts, dragons, Babylon, 666, famines, and wars) and end up feeding their fears rather than their faith. How sad! God is robbed of the glory due his name and believers are bereft of peace, joy, and hope won for them by Jesus. This just does not have to be!

There are no accidents or coincidences for the people of God. There is just God's loving, if sometimes hard to accept, providence.

Coming to accept and rest in the sovereignty of God has been a lifelong struggle of mine, starting with an episode of sexual abuse when I was just eight—a story I never voiced or dealt with until well after turning fifty. Three years later, when I was eleven, my mom was killed in a car wreck. My dad was so devasted, he didn't speak her name for the next forty years, the same amount of time it took me to return to Mom's grave.

It made no sense to me that God would leave me motherless just as I was beginning those precarious adolescent years. I lamented it then, and I lament it now. But God has, indeed, proven to me that his name is Redeemer—the God who works in *all things* for our good, and his glory. I continue to learn this lesson over and over. The Bible never states our God does all things easily, but that he does all things well. Our Father doesn't always answer our questions, but he always gives us himself.

In many seasons of life, the glorious truth of God's sovereignty has been put to the test. As a pastor, I've walked our church through the brutal murder of one of our pastors by his jealous son-in-law, the tragic death of Steven Curtis and Mary Beth Chapman's adopted daughter when her brother accidently ran over her, still-born deaths of precious image bearers of God, and suicide deaths of believers whose pain was more real than God's love in the crisis of their despair.

And just hours after I finished writing the first manuscript of *Unveiled Hope* on the Monday after Easter in 1996, I received the heart-wrenching news that my mentor and discipler for twenty-one years had been taken to heaven. Dr. Jack Miller, the man who taught me and showed me more of the grace of the gospel than anyone else, went home—to the real home. I never begrudged Jack one day in heaven, but his death happened on the cusp of my most difficult season of life, and it took years for me to recover from the resulting burnout.

And yet, how appropriate it was for Jack to die the day after we celebrated Jesus Christ's resurrection—the greatest and most loving demonstration of the sovereign mercy and might of the one upon the throne. Oh, the despair that would have filled my soul if I did not believe with every fiber of my being that God loves, and that he is in control! Thank God, there is a joyful, peaceful, and totally occupied throne in heaven.

DISCUSSION *10 minutes*

In the past, how have you felt about the Bible's descriptions of the end times? Have those descriptions tended to feed your fears or your faith? Explain.

The article mentions three wrong approaches to the troubles of life:

1. Fatalistic (whatever will be, will be)
2. Stoic (accept things without questions or complaining)
3. Superficial (deny the pain)

Which is most tempting for you, and how does it rob God of glory in your life?

Lesson

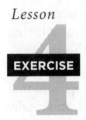

EXERCISE

GOD REIGNS

15 MINUTES

Think about the threats and evils in your life that cause you to worry, fear, be sad, or feel defeated. The message of Revelation is that your God rules over them all! He will destroy those threats and evils when, in his good plan, it is the right time to do so. This means that while these things will trouble you for now, you need not fear nor feel defeated, nor grieve as one who has no hope.

For this exercise, remind yourself that your God reigns over all that brings evil or sadness to your life. Do this by creating your own representation of God's throne room. The following page has a picture of God's throne in the center. Around it, in God's sphere of influence, are listed categories of troubles. Pick some that are true of your life. Fill in the details of that trouble or sadness. You might want to write it down in the available white space or make some other kind of note. Encircle the throne with your troubles, fears, and sadness. God rules over them all.

Who are some **seemingly powerful people who scare you?** They may be people who are . . .

At work
In your family
In your neighborhood
World leaders
National leaders
Local authorities
Other people: _____

What are some **big events that worry you?** They may involve . . .

The state of your nation
The state of the world
The state of the church
Family concerns
Financial concerns
Work concerns
Health concerns
Fears about death
Other worries: _____

What are some **sources of sadness in your life,** or **struggles that make you feel defeated?** They may involve . . .

- Death
- Family disappointments
- Unsaved people
- A sin you've not overcome
- Your spiritual life
- A personal relationship
- Your nation's direction
- The world's condition
- Other sadness/defeat: _____

What are some **things you fear doing for God?** They may involve . . .

- Leaving your "comfort zone" for the sake of others
- Telling others about Jesus
- Confronting evil
- Confessing sin
- Risking rebuke
- Risking loss of reputation
- Risk to your life
- Risk to your family
- Other fears: _____

Lesson 4: Jesus Opens Heaven's Door 43

When the group is ready, share some of your responses. What are the concerns, fears, and sadness your God is sovereign over?

Especially consider the last category of things you fear doing for God. If you had more confidence that God was in control of the first three categories—scary people, worrisome events, and sad happenings—how would it help you overcome your fear of doing hard things for God?

WRAP-UP AND PRAYER *10 minutes*

Be sure to pray about your fears, worries, and sadness. These are not things to keep *from* your God, but rather some of the chief things you should take *to* him, knowing that he loves to have you approach his throne of grace.

5

JESUS RECEIVES WORSHIP

BIG IDEA

Only Jesus was worthy to accomplish God's redemption, and only he is worthy to receive our worship. As we see him more fully, our worship becomes perfected.

BIBLE CONVERSATION *15 minutes*

As we move into Revelation 5, the heavenly worship of God shifts to focus on God's grand plan of redemption. John's vision concerns a scroll that contains God's purposes for history. But at first, no one can be found who is worthy to unseal that scroll—to reveal and unleash that wonder-filled redemption. Have someone read **Revelation 5** aloud, or have a few readers take turns. Then discuss the questions below.

Jesus is first described as the Lion of Judah in reference to his kingly pedigree (see Genesis 49:9–10, which says "the obedience of the nations will be his"). Then without warning, he becomes a slain Lamb. How does this imagery give a richer description of Jesus than plain words might give?

The new song in verses 9 and 10 is a song that spells out the gospel. What elements make up this gospel story? Why is each element critical if the gospel is to be good news to you?

This songs in the vision reveal the completion of Jesus's Great Commission to take the gospel into the whole world. Which parts of this vision most encourage you to have a role in that mission, and why?

****

Now read this lesson's article aloud, switching readers at each paragraph break. Then discuss the questions that follow the article.

THE PERFECTED WORSHIP OF HEAVEN

5 MINUTES

Since becoming a Christian, I have had the privilege of experiencing firsthand the enormity and the diversity of the body of Christ. My travel, through various missions and ministry opportunities, has been just as important to my spiritual formation as my seminary training. But through my travels, and from studying church history, it has become redundantly obvious to me that we Christians don't tend to handle our rich diversity very well at all.

Painfully and oddly, our disunity is nowhere more clearly pronounced than when the topic of worship emerges. That which is meant to be an expression of Spirit-wrought humility and the other-centered adoration of God too often becomes a battleground on which proud combatants vie for the right to define the liturgy and control the music of the worship service. More often than not, this is usually all about one's own aesthetic sensibilities and preferences. I have observed suspicion, anger, manipulation, and hostility surrounding the control of the worship service. What an ugly circumstance and utter contradiction of the nature and purpose of the worship of God! Perhaps we shouldn't be surprised, as the first "worship war" resulted in the first homicide when Cain killed his brother Abel.

Revelation confronts these sins and invites us to something far more glorious. John is given a vision of the worship of heaven. He sees and hears that for which we have been made, that which will be our sumptuous feast throughout eternity. From this point on in Revelation, we will see that the worship of the Lamb and the one upon the throne is the defining reality of the people of God. It is the means by which we are to wage war against Satan in the world, not against one another in the body of Christ.

As God is worshiped as Creator in Revelation 4, so he is worshiped as Redeemer in chapter 5. Our focus moves from the one upon the throne to the one who hung upon the cross. John looks for the Lion who can accomplish God's foreordained history, and he instead sees a Lamb. What a glorious paradox! This Lamb, "looking as if it had been slain," becomes the central figure on whom all attention is focused. Even in heaven we will be eternally reminded of the fact that it is only by virtue of Jesus's substitutionary atonement that we are there and that history has been brought to its fulfillment. He is the messianic King because he has been faithful to his calling as the Lamb of God.

This is no ordinary lamb that John sees, but one with seven horns and seven eyes. The horns should make us think of the fullness of Jesus's power, as horns are a symbol of strength in the Scriptures. The eyes show that there is nothing which Jesus does not know and there is no place where he is not! This Lamb is not lame. In one of the most dramatic and glorious events in all of history, Jesus, as the Lamb, comes and takes the scroll from the Father's right hand. Immediately, worship breaks out. The elders begin singing a new song—the song of redemption.

True worship has a way of gathering momentum and a crowd. John "looked and heard the voice of many angels, numbering thousands upon thousands, and ten thousand times ten thousand." And before long, he saw and heard "every creature in heaven and on earth and under the earth and in the sea, and all that is in them." Everyone and everything give God and the Lamb their worthy due. Oh, to be reduced to such other-centered adoration of the Lord of creation and redemption!

What effect would this vision have had on the seven churches in Asia Minor? The persecuted are deeply encouraged to endure all things on behalf of him who bore all things for their redemption. The cold-hearted are invited to be renewed in their affections for him whose love is their own rebuke. Jewish Christians are reassured that Jesus is indeed God's Messiah, the Lion of the tribe of Judah. The fearful are given confidence as they see who really controls history and their destiny. The outnumbered Christians in the Roman world are made aware that they are far from being a minority, for they are a part of an uncountable community.

Those deceived by false teaching are confronted with worship that is "in truth" and therefore pure. The spiritually dead are confronted with worship that is "in Spirit" and therefore alive. The whole church is called to affirm afresh, with confidence and passion and joy, that Jesus is Lord and God.

What about us? How should our understanding and experience of worship be shaped by what we see of God's worship in eternity? Perhaps in recent years we have unwittingly done a better job of worshiping worship than of worshiping God. As long as the discussion about worship centers on what we like or dislike, we have missed the heart of worship. The questions we should be faithfully wrestling with are: What does God desire in his worship? What is acceptable worship, according to the instruction we find in the Bible? How can we more faithfully represent, honor, and serve God in his worship? Only his glory and honor should matter to us.

William Temple once offered this comprehensive definition of worship: "Worship is the submission of all our nature to God. It is the quickening of conscience by his holiness; the nourishment of mind with his truth; the purifying of imagination by his beauty; the opening of the heart to his love; the surrender of will to his purpose—and all this gathered up in adoration, the most selfless emotion of which our nature is capable and therefore the chief remedy for that self-centeredness which is our original sin and the source of all actual sin." As it is in heaven, so may it be here!

DISCUSSION *10 minutes*

The article pointed out that worship is meant to be an expression of humility. But many of us struggle to set aside judging or complaining attitudes about the service when we come to worship. Share your experience. Why is it hard to be humble and forgiving when we worship, of all times?

How is true worship "the chief remedy for self-centeredness"? If you can, give an example from your life.

Lesson

EXERCISE

APPROACHES TO WORSHIP

20 MINUTES

Most of us already have ideas and attitudes about worship. These probably include many good attitudes, but we can always grow. This exercise looks at what we can learn about worship from the descriptions in Revelation. Work through the exercise on your own, rating yourself on how you approach or think about worship. When the group is ready, you'll discuss and share some of your answers.

Part 1: Your Approach to Worship. Consider where your approach to worship lies along the lines described below. Is it in the middle, toward one end, or at one end?

NOTE: For each of the descriptions below, the ideal, "best" answer would be to fully affirm *both* ends of the line. This exercise won't let you do that, because picking the ideal answer is not the point. By forcing yourself to choose between two good options, you will see where your approach to worship may be able to grow.

SPIRIT and TRUTH. The worship described in Revelation reflects Jesus's statement in John 4:23 that true worshipers will worship in the Spirit and in truth. SPIRIT means an inner aliveness and delight for God, avoiding dead orthodoxy. TRUTH means we care for right doctrine and celebrate Jesus for who he truly is, avoiding empty emotionalism. Which comes easiest for you?

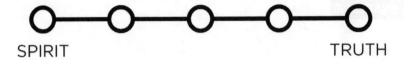

SPIRIT   TRUTH

TRANSCENDENCE and IMMANENCE. In Revelation, God is both far greater than his people and right there among his people. TRANSCENDENCE means we worship God for his above-us glory and holiness. IMMANENCE means we worship with appreciation for the intimacy of having him with us. Which do you do most readily?

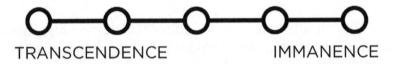

TRANSCENDENCE   IMMANENCE

MIND and BODY. The worshipers in Revelation are both mentally engaged and physically active (bowing, singing). MIND means we don't just go through the motions. BODY means we show up in person and actively take part. Which do you find easiest?

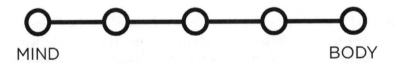

MIND   BODY

VERTICAL and HORIZONTAL. Worship is directed both "up" to God and outward to each other. VERTICAL means we focus on our relationship with God and we celebrate being reconciled with him. HORIZONTAL means worship is not about *you* but rather about *us*, and we also celebrate being reconciled with each other as we worship *together* for mutual benefit. Which do you do most readily?

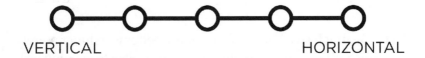

VERTICAL   HORIZONTAL

DIVERSITY and UNITY. Heavenly worship features people from every nation all praising God together for the same reasons. DIVERSITY means we are intentionally inclusive, introducing people from every nation to Jesus and worshiping with all kinds of people who are in many ways different from us. UNITY means we don't feel so different because we all share a common hope in Jesus. Which do you most easily desire?

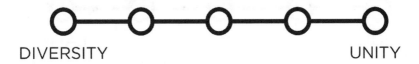

DIVERSITY   UNITY

HEART and ART. The worship in Revelation involves music and dialogue and religious objects. HEART means we don't let things like the music turn our worship into an entertainment session. ART means we do pursue excellence in using our musical gifts to praise God, lest we offer him that which cost us nothing. Which most readily matters to you?

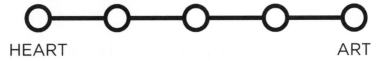

HEART   ART

LITURGY and LIFE. Worship is both a special gathering and all of life. LITURGY means we do not neglect weekly worship together. LIFE means we realize that in a sense we are still worshipers the rest of the time, always seeking to glorify God and advance his kingdom in the world. Which comes easiest for you?

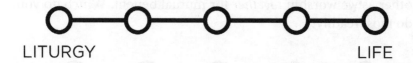

LITURGY   LIFE

Part 2: Seeing Jesus. You won't become a better worshiper merely by trying harder to make it happen. We are moved to worship well when we see Jesus, experience his love, and believe his promises. Revelation helps us to do this. It shows us Jesus as the royal LION, "the ruler of the kings of the earth" (1:4). And it also shows us Jesus as the slain LAMB, "who loves us and has freed us from our sins by his blood" (1:5).

We need to see Jesus as both **LION and LAMB**. Which comes easiest for you?

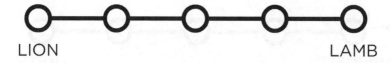

LION   LAMB

When the group is ready, share some of your results. Where might you have opportunities to enrich your worship of Jesus by approaching worship better?

Pay special attention to the final item, Jesus as Lion and Lamb. Do you tend to emphasize one of these aspects of him over the other? Explain why, if you can. How could your appreciation of Jesus grow? If it did, how might this enrich your worship?

Why do unbelievers need for us to proclaim Jesus as both Lion and Lamb?

WRAP-UP AND PRAYER *10 minutes*

Prayer is an act of worship. As you pray together, praising and thanking your God and asking him for all you need, enjoy the fact that already now you are in some sense participating in the glorious scene described in Revelation 4 and 5.

Lesson

6

JESUS BRINGS PURPOSE TO OUR SUFFERING

BIG IDEA

Our suffering in this world is under God's control. It has meaning and a tender, redemptive purpose: God plans to wipe away every tear from our eyes.

BIBLE CONVERSATION *20 MINUTES*

Chapter 5 ended with the worthy Lamb, Jesus, ready to open the seven seals. These seals are the first of several series to come in Revelation that picture, in vivid episodes, the story of life on earth between Jesus's first and second comings. As you read this lesson's passage, you'll see that the first four seals seem to describe the sufferings of this world: war, violence, economic oppression, and death. The fifth seal describes the persecution of God's people. The sixth describes the terror of the judgment of evil God's people have been awaiting, and the seventh finally brings the silence of godly awe.

Have several readers take turns reading **Revelation 6 and 7**. Then discuss the questions below:

Look at how verses 1–11 of chapter 6 describe life in the world. Which part most causes you to say, "Yes, that bothers me about the world," and why?

Compare the fate of those who refuse to humble themselves before God at the end of chapter 6 with the ending for believers in chapter 7. What differences do you most notice? Are there similarities too?

****

Now read the following article together. Take turns reading aloud, switching readers at each paragraph break.

THE LAST DAYS

5 MINUTES

When are the last days? When I became a Christian in 1968, it was assumed that we were living in the last days and that they only began rather recently, as in the beginning of the '60s. According to Scripture, however, the last days have been going on for quite a while. The apostle Peter stood up on Pentecost and announced that the coming of the Spirit signaled that the last days had begun: "In the last days, God says, I will pour out my Spirit on all people" (Acts 2:17). And Hebrews says, "In these last days [God] has spoken to us by his Son" (Hebrews 1:2). This means the entire period between the first and second comings of Jesus should be viewed as the last days.

Revelation is a last-days manual for the whole people of God. The several scenes presented in chapters 6 through 22 are a series of repeating episodes—gracious gifts of God informing, warning, and encouraging us about things that have been, things that are, and things that are to come. The same events and timeline are viewed, and then viewed again, from different perspectives. Here we see the Christian life as it will be until Jesus returns. It has been and it will be full of rapture and rupture. And Jesus is thoroughly in control of all things, including the suffering of his people.

If the first four seals in chapter 6 symbolize life in a fallen world for all the citizens of the earth, then the fifth seal focuses on life for Christians during this same timeframe. Suffering, including the suffering of martyrdom, is very much a part of the abundant life Jesus has won for his people. The apostle Paul wrote, "For it has been granted to you on behalf of Christ not only to believe on him, but also to suffer for him" (Philippians 1:29). The Greek text literally says suffering has been "grace-gifted."

How many of us consider suffering a blessing, an actual expression of the grace of God? We live in a day in which the gospel has been so corrupted that there are those who literally teach that the only reason Christians suffer is because of a *lack* of faith. What an affront this is to the thousands of Christians who die every year only because of the faith! There were more Christian martyrs in the twentieth century than the combined total in the previous nineteen centuries. The fifth seal brings encouragement to Christians of every generation and place in the world.

God answers his people's cry by calling them to "wait a little longer, until the full number of their fellow servants, their brothers and sisters, were killed just as they had been" (6:11). What a profoundly encouraging word from our Father! God is not only in control of the seasons but also of our sufferings, even over the specific number of martyrs.

Before the breaking of the seventh seal, John is given a glimpse of the totality of redeemed humanity, symbolized by a number whose multiples are twelve times twelve times one thousand. Once again, God is worshiped as the one who has loved his people well through the entirety of tribulation. In Revelation, tribulation is not viewed simply as the final outburst of suffering of the people of God previous to the return of Jesus. Rather, it is the totality of pain, suffering, persecution, and sorrow that we experience in this fallen, God-hating world.

Then John is given one of the most inviting pictures of life in heaven for the people of God. With our brothers and sisters from throughout the history of redemption, we will be "before the throne of God and serve him day and night in his temple." And consider how we will be loved and cared for in our eternal abode: All hunger and thirst are over, forever! Our Lamb has become our Shepherd. Even in heaven, Jesus will be ministering to us, loving us, leading us. Eternal refreshment and the redeeming of all of our tears will be our great joy and satisfaction. This is the fulfillment of everything promised in the name *Immanuel*—"God with us."

All of God's providences and sovereign dealings will become clear to us. Even the things we have despised most, that have caused us to question the mercy and might of God, will be resolved. I strongly suspect (but don't quote me on this!) that for the first thousand years in heaven we are going to hear echoing throughout our Father's house: "Oh, so *that's* what you were doing! Now I see it. Now I understand. Father, your ways were not always easy but now I see your glory in all that you did, and I praise you for being so incalculably good and wise."

DISCUSSION *10 minutes*

Why is it important for you to realize and expect that God has planned both "rapture and rupture" for your life in this world?

In what ways have you begun to see how suffering in your life has been an expression of God's grace to you?

Lesson

EXERCISE

USING THE BIBLE TO REFLECT ON SUFFERING

15 MINUTES

The line that says God will wipe away every tear from our eyes is strikingly intimate. It doesn't merely say God will get rid of tears and crying. Instead, it describes a tender act in which he personally comforts his grieving people, as a parent might with a sobbing child. The imagery invites us to think deeply about God's plan for the end of suffering.

This is typical of the Bible. It gives deep, not simplistic, answers to the very real problem of suffering in the world. For this exercise, work on your own to consider how this lesson's passage begins to address some of our responses to suffering.

Step 1. From the list below, select a suffering response to think about. It may be a response you have had either to the troubles of life or to some suffering that's resulted from serving God and a life on mission for him. Or it may be a response you've seen in others. (All the responses on this list are common human responses to suffering. God does not condemn us for feeling them—they are found in the Psalms and other places in the Bible—but rather

61

invites us to come to him in faith and spend a lifetime working through them with him.)

☐ "This is just too hard. I can't keep going."

☐ "This is just too sad. I can't keep taking it."

☐ "If God is good and in charge of the world, why would he let this happen?"

☐ "This feels purposeless. It would really help to know how this is part of God's plan. Can't he give me some clues?"

☐ "I'm tired. I want out."

☐ "I hear talk of victory in Christ, but this doesn't feel like victory. Something isn't working right. Either I'm doing it wrong, or God is wrong."

☐ "If this is God's plan for me, I'm not sure I like God."

☐ "None of this is making me feel closer to God, or more repentant, or more faithful. Maybe God has no plans to save me or be good to me at all, ever."

☐ "I didn't do anything to deserve this."

☐ "Too much about this world seems unfair. It's not right!"

☐ "It's taking too long. I want answers/justice/relief now."

☐ "I shouldn't have to bear all of this. God expects too much."

☐ "I'm getting jaded. I expected better out of life and from God."

☐ "I'm having doubts. Is God's kingdom really advancing? I know the Bible says it is, but it feels like evil is in total control."

☐ Other: _____.

Step 2. Take several minutes to quietly reflect. Ask yourself: How does today's passage, and Revelation 7:17 in particular, start to address the response to suffering that you picked in step 1?

> "For the Lamb at the center of the throne
> will be their shepherd;
> 'he will lead them to springs of living water.'
> 'And God will wipe away every tear from their eyes.'"
> (Revelation 7:17)

When the group is ready, share some of your thoughts. What response did you pick, and what are some of your initial reflections? Can you see how deeper reflection might be profitable?

WRAP-UP AND PRAYER *10 minutes*

Prayer is one way God invites us to come to him in faith with our questions and feelings that flow from suffering. Take time to do that as a group now.

ASSIGNMENT: The next lesson will cover chapters 8 through 10 of Revelation. That's too much to read during group time, so you will be reading only chapter 10 when you meet as a group. To prepare for the lesson, please read **Revelation 8 and 9** on your own before you meet next time. That passage is about a series of seven trumpets and the judgment they announce. It may help for you to think of the seven trumpets as similar to the seven seals. If the seven seals represent God's plan for his people in the last days, the seven trumpets represent his partial judgment on unbelievers in the last days.

Lesson

7

THE LAST CHANCE TO BELIEVE IN JESUS

BIG IDEA

These troubled last days come with a glorious and mighty call for all the nations to believe the gospel.

BIBLE CONVERSATION *20 MINUTES*

Let's review the landscape of the part of Revelation we are in:

- Chapters 6 and 7 (our last lesson): The seven seals show that difficult times mark the last days for the people of God.

- Chapters 8 and 9 (your at-home reading): The seven trumpets that follow show that difficult times mark the last days for unbelievers. People had better come to their senses and repent during these days of partial judgment and continuing mercy, for final justice is coming.

- Chapter 10 (this lesson's group-time reading): Before the final trumpet sounds, there is a last call. The inhabitants of the earth who have seen the horrors God can bring should heed the call of his mighty angel and believe the gospel while there is still time.

With that framework in place, have someone read **Revelation 10** aloud. Then discuss the questions that follow:

How are the kinds of worldwide troubles described in chapters 8 and 9 a wake-up call for people to turn to God? Would people be more or less likely to seek God if there were fewer calamities? Why or why not?

Ezekiel 3 describes the word of God as a sweet-tasting scroll, so the angel with the scroll seems to be a picture about God's gospel message for the world. How does the paradox in the vision—an impressive angel with an unimpressive scroll—fit the proclamation of the gospel? (Consider both how it fits those who proclaim the gospel and how it fits the message itself.)

In what ways is the word of God both sweet and somehow sour? Have you tasted this experience? How?

****

Now read aloud the article, "Justice Is Coming," taking turns by paragraph, and discuss the questions that follow it.

Lesson 7: The Last Chance to Believe in Jesus **65**

Lesson

ARTICLE

JUSTICE IS COMING

5 MINUTES

Some of the hardest realities for Christians to accept are those seasons and situations in which God, who reveals himself as being both mighty and merciful, appears to be neither. In recent years, my wife has walked with courageous women coming to Jesus after spending years as sexual slaves in the dark world of human trafficking and more years in prison, paying the price for their addiction to drugs—the pernicious tool of their pimps. Where was God in their season of being preyed upon by evil and sold into slavery?

This is just one of countless stories I could tell—and you could tell—of the apparent injustice of life in a world over which we are told God absolutely reigns. Yet God tells these stories too. One of God's great gifts to us is the honesty of his written Word. The Bible is the original and only no-spin zone. God has not edited out the many, many stories of how his people have been vexed and angered at the unfairness of life and the silence of God in the face of those who despise his name and reject his authority. How can evil prevail and even seem to prosper?

To such an ongoing theological conundrum, the seven trumpets speak. Justice is coming, both for the people of God and for those who despise the mercy and grace of God. The blast of the trumpets should encourage God's people who painfully wonder at his timetable. Perhaps we would be right to call this season of the Christian life the "wait of grace." God promises us sufficient grace as we long for justice, even as he extends grace to those who have reviled him and caused great suffering for his people. God doesn't work by our schedule, but evil and suffering do have an expiration date.

It is helpful to consider Paul's teaching on this same topic. He wrote, "The wrath of God is being revealed from heaven against all the godlessness and wickedness of people, who suppress the truth by their wickedness, since what may be known about God is plain to them, because God has made it plain to them" (Romans 1:18–19).

And later, "Do you show contempt for the riches of his kindness, forbearance and patience, not realizing that God's kindness is intended to lead you to repentance? But because of your stubbornness and your unrepentant heart, you are storing up wrath against yourself for the day of God's wrath, when his righteous judgment will be revealed" (Romans 2:4–5).

Paul argues that even as judgment is coming with the full fury of the holiness of God, so judgment is already being revealed from heaven. All around us, God is demonstrating that he is not winking at sin—even as his days of mercy linger. We Christians are tempted to believe that God is slow to hear our prayers and slow to avenge his glory. Unbelievers are tempted to be presumptuous about God's promise to bring judgment, showing contempt for the patience that is meant to lead them to repent.

Consider how the seven trumpets speak to both of these groups. As with the seven seals, so we see a natural division. The first four trumpets largely show the effects of God's present judgment on the inanimate world. The last three trumpets demonstrate his judgment on the people who inhabit it. We can see parallels between these judgments and those God visited on the Egyptians during the time of the exodus. The greater exodus from sin and death, effected by King Jesus, is accompanied by God's judgments now as well.

- With the first trumpet blast, the earth is stricken and the environment affected. What we call natural disasters are to be seen as God getting our attention.

- With the second trumpet blast, the sea is stricken and commerce affected. Sometimes the only thing seemingly capable of redirecting the minds and hearts of unbelievers toward heaven is for their money supply to be shaken.

- With the third trumpet blast, the rivers are stricken and natural resources affected. God can take from natural water its power to satisfy our thirst, so that a deeper thirst for the living water of the gospel might be quickened.

- With the fourth trumpet blast, the sky is stricken and humanity's vision affected. God will intensify the darkness so as to create a longing for the true Light.

- With the fifth trumpet, Satan emerges as an instrument of God's judgment against the stubborn and rebellious who continue to refuse the warnings and wooings of the living God.

- With the sixth trumpet, angels and horsemen are released. Tragically, as after the other trumpets, we see pain but no repentance: "The rest of mankind who were not killed by these plagues still did not repent of the work of their hands" (9:20). What an indictment against the foolish hearts of men! Nothing is left but final judgment to be seen in the blowing of the seventh trumpet.

But before the last trumpet is blown, an incredibly large and splendid angel appears with legs that straddle the earth and the sea. Many believe him to represent the worldwide spread of the gospel, and the scroll to be the Word of God "with the message of salvation in Christ on every page."[1] This is the only escape on judgment day—to have believed the gospel!

The angel announces that God will delay no longer. The epoch of mercy is about to give way to the day of justice. John is

---

1. Chuck Colclasure, *The Overcomers* (Nashville: Thomas Nelson, 1981), 101.

told to eat the scroll, a reminder of the prophet Ezekiel's experience of eating the bittersweet word of God. Yes, the gospel and the Christian life contain things both pleasant and difficult. But both are a part of the good plan of God, who still today holds out his glorious gospel.

DISCUSSION *10 minutes*

How have you personally seen troubling events turn someone,,or yourself, back to God?

There have been sad instances of believers pointing to a disaster or evil event and, without any compassion, declaring it to be God's judgment on those who suffered. How can you affirm that God *is* giving the world a preview of his wrath, as Romans 1 says, but that his purposes remain compassionate? What words might you use to explain this?

THE BITTERSWEET GOSPEL

15 MINUTES

The vision of the massive angel standing over the earth ought to impress us with the grandeur of the Great Commission Jesus has given us—to urgently proclaim the gospel to the whole world in these last days. We invite people everywhere to trust Christ as their Savior. And we demonstrate the love of God and his emerging kingdom by loving others and working with God to restore what is broken in the world. Yes, God sends disasters. But he also sends his people with a still-in-time message of love and hope as magnificent as the angel's great roar.

Though this gospel at its core is "good news," its taste is not all sweetness when we chew on it a bit. The joy of salvation comes with the sad realization that those who reject Jesus face his judgment, and the thrill of living for Jesus comes with sacrifice and often hardship. So, as we go about this mission, we are motivated by both the sweet and bitter sides of the gospel we proclaim, and the mission itself at times tastes sweet and at other times bitter. It helps to be aware of this and discuss it with other believers.

For this exercise, first work on your own to complete some of the following sentences about mission and the gospel (don't feel you necessarily have to complete every one). When the group is ready, share and discuss some of your responses.

A **SWEET** gospel truth that I love to tell to others is _____
_____
_____.

A **BITTER** situation that gives me urgency to tell the gospel, or to help others in Jesus's name, is _____
_____.

A **SWEET** way Jesus has loved me that makes me want to love others is _____
_____.

A **BITTER** hardship that comes with laying down my life for others, and makes me hesitant to go out on mission, is _____
_____
_____.

A **SWEET** assurance I have in Jesus, which encourages me when loving others gets hard and feels bitter, is _____
_____
_____.

Now tell the group some of your responses. How does the sweetness of the gospel message, and the bitterness that results when it is not heard or believed, motivate you?

How do you react to the sweetness and bitterness of life and of mission? What kind of character and habits should mark the mission work of one who knows both the sweetness and the bitterness?

WRAP-UP AND PRAYER *10 minutes*

In your prayer time together, you might include prayer for those who have not yet believed the gospel.

Lesson

8

WITNESSING FOR JESUS

BIG IDEA

Even though it brings opposition that may seem for a while to humiliate us or bring us death, our witness for Jesus has powerful impact in these last days, and will end in glory.

BIBLE CONVERSATION *15 minutes*

As we move into Revelation 11, we are still on the cusp of the seventh and final trumpet of judgment. Again, the church's witness to the nations has a role to play before the end comes. As you read, you will encounter some imagery that may benefit from brief explanations:

- There is a period of three and a half years, and another of three and a half days. Whether this refers to actual years and days either in the past or in the future, or to the entire time period between Christ's first and second comings, or to both, the number three and a half in Revelation and in the book of Daniel consistently denotes a period when evil seems to reign but also a period that is limited, being only half of a seven-year sabbath cycle.

- There are two witnesses represented as olive trees and lamp-stands. We've already seen in chapter 1 that lampstands represent Christ's church, and in Zechariah 4, two olive trees represent those who serve the Lord. The number two may have a pair of specific gospel preachers in mind, or it may signify that their testimony is trustworthy since they corroborate each other, a rule established in Deuteronomy 19:15.

Now have someone read **Revelation 11** aloud, or have a few readers take turns. Then discuss the following questions:

Describe the ups and downs of the ministry of the two witnesses. When do things look most dire, and when do the witnesses have the most impact?

How might that same cycle of ups and downs fit the life of anyone who professes Christ?

Look at the heavenly proclamation in verse 15. What are some of the many reasons why this coming event was good news to John's persecuted readers in the Roman Empire, and also is good news to you today?

∗∗∗∗

Now read the article that goes with this lesson, and discuss the
questions that follow it.

Lesson

OUT OF THE BOMB SHELTER

5 MINUTES

Billy Hartman was one of my good buddies growing up. He lived on a big farm with horses, only a ten-minute walk from my home. One of the most profound memories I have of the Hartman farm and family was the time they installed the first bomb shelter I had ever seen. It was during the Cuban Missile Crisis, when the Cold War seemed ready to lead us into the first all-out nuclear war. In that atmosphere of real fear, the bomb-shelter business thrived.

However, this was not the last time I experienced a bomb-shelter mentality. The second was spiritual, generated by the threat of the Antichrist. A lot more fear than faith was generated in my heart, and in many of my late-60s Christian counterparts, by prophecy mongers whose popularity was only exceeded by the growth of their seminars and book sales. The net effect of those who made their living by feeding our phobias was the retreat of Christians from the culture into little ecclesiastical bomb shelters.

Christian communes were planned. Food stuffs were stockpiled. Warnings were issued against owning anything with the number 666 on it. Guessing the identity of the Antichrist became a growing sport among those who were becoming less and less engaged with the world—the world into which we have been commissioned as witnesses and kingdom representatives until King Jesus returns. It really makes me both mad and sad as I look back over those days. This is just the opposite effect that the book of Revelation is meant to have.

In Revelation 11, we meet the two witnesses who are raised up and empowered by God for faithful and effective ministry during a persecution-filled period. As they continue their ministry among the nations, John records a fatal attack—but only after "they have finished their testimony." Satan's attack cannot alter that which our Father has purposed. The gospel *is* running through the nations. There *will* be men and women from every people group populating the new heaven and new earth. This is no mere possibility or probability, but a God-promised actuality. The kingdom of the world *will* become the kingdom of our Lord and of his Messiah, and he will reign for ever and ever!

The attack on the witnesses leads to their deaths and a brief period of gloating. But what seemed to be the death of the witnesses actually gives rise to their resurrection and glory. The beast's victory is hollow! God's enemies are startled, humbled, and overwhelmed when he vindicates his servants.

As the people of God, we are known, numbered, loved, and protected against all ultimate harm and loss. We are not to develop a bomb-shelter mentality even in the face of great opposition and persecution. Our calling has never been to retreat into little Christian cocoons of fear, self-protection, and survival. Although there will be times and places in which it seems the church has been silenced and defeated, the demise is only brief and apparent. The blood of the martyrs has always proven to be the seed of the church. The enemies of God may have a seasonal laugh, but the loudest and longest laugh comes from heaven:

> The One enthroned in heaven laughs;
>   the Lord scoffs at them.
> He rebukes them in his anger

> and terrifies them in his wrath, saying,
> "I have installed my king
>   on Zion, my holy mountain." (Psalm 2:4–6)

Our calling is not to waste time trying to run from credit cards with 666 on them. We are, by our proclamation and by our presence, to preach and demonstrate the gospel of Jesus Christ among the nations until he comes back. We, the church, are the two witnesses. We are empowered by God himself. He is the Lord of both miracles and persecutions, both gospel advancements and apparent gospel setbacks.

The missionary who may see one convert in ten years is neither a failure nor ineffective. God alone is the one who faithfully applies the saving benefits of Jesus Christ to the lost. The gospel goes forth both in blessing and judgment. It is up to the Lord of the harvest how this mystery is played out. Our calling is not to be "successful," but faithful.

What are we afraid of? This is our Father's world. No one will ultimately thwart his ways. No, we are not to be naïve about life in "Sodom and Egypt." In fact, the coming chapters of Revelation have much to teach us about living wisely in the world. But we are given insight about real-world hardships so we can have confidence and hope as we seek to live out the radical implications of the gospel in the context of evil Babylon. Each of us needs to be far more taken up with the glory and grace of our sovereign God, and surrendered to his purposes in his world.

With the blowing of the seventh trumpet we are introduced to the end of the ages as we know them. This is the final day, the day of the Lord! This vision is the fulfillment of the great promise of a King whose increase and whose peace will know no end. This King Jesus will reign for ever and ever. Every time I sing this great passage set to music in Handel's *Messiah*, I am simply overwrought. Every longing in my soul is ignited at the anticipation of this awesome and glorious day.

DISCUSSION *10 minutes*

In what ways have you been a bomb-shelter believer, and in what other ways have you ventured out of your bunker?

When you think of your own life cycle, how much do you see it as a pattern of death to be followed by resurrection? What difference does that way of thinking make in how you live?

Lesson

EXERCISE

GO AND DIE

20 MINUTES

The bomb-shelter illustration is helpful because, for a believer, coming out of the bunker means death. Yet that is what we do: we go out on mission. Whether you cross the street or cross the world, and whether it is to tell about Jesus or to display his kingdom through kindness, doing this in love will mean a sort of dying. You might not meet physical death (though you might, to be followed someday by resurrection!), but you will have to die in some way.

On your own, read the descriptions of the ways God calls us to die. Also read the Bible assurances of ultimate victory that come with each. (Your dying is not defeat, but rather the path to true impact as a witness for your Savior.) Consider how God is calling you to die. Pick a category, or think of a specific example if you can, and be prepared to share when the group is ready.

TYPE OF DEATH	BIBLE'S ASSURANCE OF ULTIMATE VICTORY
Risk of physical death and persecution. To go out on mission or, sometimes, simply to acknowledge our allegiance to Jesus could subject us to loss due to persecution.	"Who shall separate us from the love of Christ? Shall trouble or hardship or persecution or famine or nakedness or danger or sword?...No, in all these things we are more than conquerors through him who loved us" (Romans 8:35, 37).
Death to a grip on our possessions. To follow Jesus on mission will mean being ready to leave behind things we love.	"Everyone who has left houses or brothers or sisters or father or mother or wife or children or fields for my sake will receive a hundred times as much and will inherit eternal life" (Matthew 19:29).
Death to comforts. Loving others and telling about Jesus will take us into uncomfortable places and situations.	"Set your minds on things above, not on earthly things. For you died, and your life is now hidden with Christ in God. When Christ, who is your life, appears, then you also will appear with him in glory" (Colossians 3:2–4).
Death to sin. The whole Christian life means killing off selfish sins. Going out to love others will surely challenge us this way.	"Wash your hands, you sinners, and purify your hearts, you double-minded. Grieve, mourn and wail. Change your laughter to mourning and your joy to gloom. Humble yourselves before the Lord, and he will lift you up" (James 4:6–10).
Death to putting ourselves first. Jesus said those who are greatest in his kingdom will conduct themselves as if they were the least.	"Humility is the fear of the LORD; its wages are riches and honor and life" (Proverbs 22:4).
Death to remaining uninvolved. It's hard to love others from a safe distance. We will have to bear their burdens alongside of them.	"Invite the poor, the crippled, the lame, the blind, and you will be blessed. Although they cannot repay you, you will be repaid at the resurrection of the righteous" (Luke 14:13–14).
Death to self-sufficiency. It is not possible to do these things in our own strength. We will have to give up our pride and rely on God.	"I will boast all the more gladly about my weaknesses, so that Christ's power may rest on me. That is why, for Christ's sake, I delight in weaknesses, in insults, in hardships, in persecutions, in difficulties. For when I am weak, then I am strong" (2 Corinthians 12:9–10).

Now share some of your thoughts. Which of the ways God calls you to die especially makes an impact on you? What might the details look like in your life?

You are not blazing new territory in this life of death. Jesus has already left his home in heaven and gone out to you, creating an example for you to follow. His was a life of service and death, leading to ultimate vindication and glory:

> He made himself nothing
>   by taking the very nature of a servant,
>   being made in human likeness.
> And being found in appearance as a man,
>   he humbled himself
>   by becoming obedient to death—
>   even death on a cross!
> Therefore God exalted him to the highest place
>   and gave him the name that is above every name,
> that at the name of Jesus every knee should bow,
>   in heaven and on earth and under the earth,
> and every tongue acknowledge that Jesus Christ is Lord,
>   to the glory of God the Father. (Philippians 2:7–11)

Why does it matter that God's call to die includes Jesus's example, and that his own death was a death *for you*?

WRAP-UP AND PRAYER *10 minutes*

A cross-shaped life of dying to self requires God's work in you.
Pray together for that grace to work in you and in each other.

Lesson

9

JESUS DEFEATS THE DEVIL

BIG IDEA

Until Jesus returns, the Christian life includes spiritual warfare. Our adversary pursues us, and we must be ready both to fight in Christ's strength and flee (retreat, harbor, abide?) to the place of his protection.

BIBLE CONVERSATION *20 MINUTES*

With chapter 12, the vision in Revelation shifts to an imagery-rich retelling of the Bible's grand story about God redeeming his people. It is the familiar story of Christmas, with references to the blood of Good Friday and the joy of Easter, leading into the centuries that follow as God's people continue to live in the world after Jesus has returned to heaven. But it is told from a heavenly perspective, as if an angel who fought the hidden battles behind the scenes were reporting on what happened from his vantage point. There are three main characters in this drama: God's people are pictured as a woman. The devil is a dragon. And Jesus is the woman's son, the child of Bethlehem we all adore.

Have someone read **Revelation 12** aloud, or have a few readers take turns. Then discuss the questions below:

The rest of the New Testament also tells the story of how Jesus was born, defeated the devil, and returned to heaven while his church remains on earth. What about Revelation's perspective do you find familiar, and what is new? What do you appreciate about this perspective, and why?

What do we learn that's important to know about the character, tactics, and motives of our adversary, the devil?

Based on the vision in this chapter, what can we expect a typical Christian life to include? How might it differ from how some people you know expect a Christian life should feel?

****

Next, take turns reading aloud the article, "God's Perspective." Then discuss the questions at the end of the article.

ARTICLE

GOD'S PERSPECTIVE

5 MINUTES

Perspective is often the only difference between paralyzing fear and liberating faith. In Revelation 12, we are invited to view what few earth dwellers could ever hope to see. God pushes back the curtains and lets us peer backstage to know what is really going on behind all the flurry and fury of the human drama. We are given priceless insight into the nature of spiritual warfare. God gives us this holy privilege that we might be filled with hope as we assume our role in his sovereign plans and purposes.

After telling the story of Jesus's birth and how he returned to heaven, John sets the scenario for the unfolding of the whole inter-advent drama—life between the two comings of Jesus. The church will be in the desert for three and a half years—a troubling but limited period of time. The period between the two comings of Christ will be full of conflict in an evil world. But God will protect and provide for his people and safeguard them against all ultimate harm.

Satan's defeat by the Lord Jesus is presented in graphic language. The vision points out how Jesus doomed the devil by his shed blood. The dragon and his allies simply are not strong enough to prevail against the hosts of heaven. Satan, who seeks to lead the whole world astray, is hurled down by King Jesus. There is already much rejoicing in heaven over the defeat dealt to Satan by the Son. Let us, therefore, rejoice too. But let us also be wise. For Satan, knowing that he is defeated and his time is short, is going down swinging, literally. His massive dragon tail is swinging wildly and destructively, for he is filled with fury.

Having failed to destroy the Son, Satan spends the rest of his days seeking to destroy the sons and daughters of the living God. How predictable it is to see that Satan's hatred of Jesus is now turned toward those whom Jesus loves, his bride. The devil knows that our destiny is most glorious, and therefore he will do anything in his power to make life miserable for us now. This is the essence of spiritual warfare: the hatred our vanquished adversary has for Jesus is now marshaled against us, the followers of the Lamb.

Jesus told us to expect trouble in this world—great trouble. But we are borne up and along as on eagles' wings. Satan will spew a river of evil at us, but God will protect and provide for us. He will never fail us. He will never leave or forsake us.

How different this perspective on spiritual warfare is from much of what I see among Christians in my American culture. On one hand, I see a lot of doubt, fear, suspicion, sensationalism, and uncertainty. The way many Christians live, one would wonder if the news ever reached them that Jesus has already won the victory over Satan. The first great promise of the gospel in Genesis 3:15, with the curse on the serpent that "he will crush your head," has been realized! We overcome him today, daily, by the blood of the Lamb—by the finished work of the Lord Jesus upon his cross. And we overcome him by the word of our testimony: by how we receive the gospel, believe it, and live it out every day until we are in heaven. We prevail because Jesus has prevailed.

But just like there are many Christians who err on the side of unbelief and fear, so there are also many who err on the opposite side of naïveté and presumption. Satan has been conquered, but not eradicated. A helpful way of thinking of Satan's defeat and the limitations of his authority over believers is to envision him on death row, held now on an unbreakable chain. A life of grace and wisdom requires that we do not venture within the length of the chain which binds our enemy. In the words of the apostle Paul, we need to be wise "in order that Satan might not outwit us. For we are not unaware of his schemes" (2 Corinthians 2:11). Indeed, much of the remainder of Revelation is written to help us see and avoid his schemes.

DISCUSSION *10 minutes*

What difference does it make for you to know that temptation is not a sign of spiritual failure but rather a sign that Satan is angry about what Jesus has done for you?

Are you more likely to forget that the devil has been overcome or to forget that you still need to flee the devil constantly?

Lesson

EXERCISE

9

FIGHT AND FLEE

15 MINUTES

Revelation's vivid picture of spiritual warfare shows us how to approach temptation in these days while Satan still pursues us. We must not err by fear, nor by presumption. Rather, we must both FIGHT and FLEE, and we must do so by FAITH in our Savior.

Work through this exercise on your own. As you go, note some of the common kinds of wrong thinking you might say to yourself to avoid fighting or fleeing. There's also a way to begin exercising faith. When the group is ready, you'll share some of your responses.

FAILING TO FIGHT

Our adversary's defeat means we have the upper hand in spiritual warfare. In Christ, we have the power to resist him. But Satan would like to keep us thinking he is too strong for us. He wants us to quickly give in to his temptations, believe his accusations, and live in fear.

When we fail to fight, we might tell ourselves something defeatist like . . .

❐ "I've tried, but I can't defeat this sin in my life. I might as well just give in."

❏ "I gave up a long time ago. I'm tired of fighting that urge. It owns me."

❏ "My sinful habits aren't changing, so I guess God just made me this way."

❏ "My sin runs too deep. God is going to be disappointed in me no matter what."

❏ "Having to repent of the same sin again and again makes me feel like a fraud. God surely is tired of hearing it or helping me."

❏ "I'm waiting for my heart to be in it. Why bother if God hasn't given me the heart for it?"

❏ "If God is behind this effort, I expect things to go swimmingly. If there's opposition, it must mean God is 'closing the door' and I should do something else."

❏ "That opportunity looks dangerous and difficult. It's probably not a good stewardship of God-given resources."

❏ Other: _____

FAILING TO FLEE

As important as it is to fight, Revelation 12 mainly shows *our role in spiritual warfare as being to flee*. We must be ever-wary of the furious dragon so that we run to places where God will protect us. Our adversary would like us to forget what danger we are in from sin, and to think we have little to fear from him and no need for God's help.

When we fail to flee, we might tell ourselves something presumptuous like . . .

❏ "What do you mean, there's sin in my life? I'm doing just fine."

❒ "I have enough willpower to handle this temptation. I don't need to run to Jesus for help."

❒ "What I'm doing isn't really wholesome, but I've decided it doesn't cross the line—at least not too far."

❒ "Sure, other people get tempted by _____, but I don't really get tempted that way. It's okay for me."

❒ "Most Christians I know do it, so it can't be that bad."

❒ "I don't want to be legalistic, or come off as critical and uptight."

❒ "I'm just exercising my Christian liberty."

❒ "I'm being transparent. I admit I struggle with the sin of _____ (meaning, I don't really struggle or flee, I just regularly give in)."

❒ "I feel a need to prove to God that I can overcome this temptation/fear on my own."

❒ "I already go to church and try to be basically good. Do I really need to fight *every* sin? I can live with a little sin. Everyone has some sin."

❒ "There's grace for me, so what's the problem?"

❒ Other: _____

FAITH

The answer to any of these excuses or feelings of failure is NOT merely to get over them and try harder, but to run to Jesus for help. Remember the true nature of spiritual warfare as pictured in Revelation: you are being pursued by Satan and you need God's help. Jesus is bigger than any of these excuses or feelings of failure. He is the source of your power. He is full of compassion when you are constantly pursued by sin. *He* keeps you fighting and keeps you safe.

One way Jesus does this is through his Word. So, read again the song of triumph from Revelation 12. Pick out some lines (perhaps underline or circle them) that will encourage you to keep fighting sin and keep fleeing to Jesus.

> "Now have come the salvation and the power
>   and the kingdom of our God,
>   and the authority of his Messiah.
> For the accuser of our brothers and sisters,
>   who accuses them before our God day and night,
>   has been hurled down.
> They triumphed over him
>   by the blood of the Lamb
>   and by the word of their testimony;
> they did not love their lives so much
>   as to shrink from death.
> Therefore rejoice, you heavens
>   and you who dwell in them!
> But woe to the earth and the sea,
>   because the devil has gone down to you!
> He is filled with fury,
>   because he knows that his time is short." (Revelation 12:10–12)

When the group is ready, share and discuss some of your responses. Be sure to include the FAITH element—the way you chose to look to Jesus through the song of triumph.

WRAP-UP AND PRAYER *10 minutes*

 Along with God's Word, prayer is a way to exercise faith in the fight against sin. Begin by praying now for protection and for strength to fight.

Lesson

10

JESUS AND HIS PERSECUTED PEOPLE

BIG IDEA

Beastly nations and philosophies threaten to dominate the world, but the gospel of Jesus still advances.

BIBLE CONVERSATION *20 MINUTES*

Our last chapter in Revelation ended with Satan, pictured as an angry dragon, bent on harassing God's people. In this lesson's passage, the dragon gives rise to two beasts he uses to carry out his plan to persecute believers.

1. There is a BEAST FROM THE SEA, reminiscent of the four beasts in Daniel 7 that represent world powers. It helps to think of this beast as representing <u>powerful governments and institutions</u> that demand allegiance in place of God and persecute those who won't comply.

2. There is a BEAST FROM THE EARTH that Revelation later labels a false prophet (in 16:13). It helps to think of this beast as representing <u>evil philosophies and false religions</u> that work in tandem with the first beast to discredit believers and make life difficult for them.

The two beasts may think they are in total control, dominating both land and sea, but there is a surprise awaiting them at the end of today's reading—if they look up! Have a few readers take turns reading **Revelation 13:1–14:13** aloud. Then discuss the questions below:

What characteristics of the two beasts fit what you have observed from world powers and false philosophies? Explain.

What parts of the vision of the Lamb and of the three angels encourage you to be involved in proclaiming the gospel to the world, and why?

✳✳✳✳

Now take turns reading the article aloud, switching readers at each paragraph break. When you finish, discuss the questions that follow.

Lesson

ARTICLE

THE BEAST'S WAY
AND THE LAMB'S WAY

5 MINUTES

We have come to one of the most sensational and hotly debated symbols in the book of Revelation. The earth beast forced everyone to receive a mark in order to buy or sell. John comments, "This calls for wisdom. Let the person who has insight calculate the number of the beast, for it is the number of a man. That number is 666" (13:18).

Who is this personification of evil symbolized by the number 666? Through the years there have been many attempts to identify the person. By using the practice of assigning a numeric significance to letters of either the Greek or Hebrew alphabet, many have qualified for this dishonor: Caesar, Nero, Martin Luther, various Popes, and many others. Take your pick! But perhaps we have been asking the wrong question. Maybe we should ask *what* this number signifies, rather than only who, for John simply says that the number stands for the beast.

Philip Hughes helps us here: "The one clue that St. John gives is that the number of the beast, 666, is the 'number of man.' The number six has understandably been regarded as a symbol of man, in that it falls short of seven, which is the divine number. On this basis the threefold six may be understood as indicative of a human

95

or humanistic trinity, that is to say a counterfeit of the divine Trinity, with all the pretensions to supreme power and authority that such a counterfeit implies."[2]

Therefore, 666 shows up in every generation and every place throughout the whole period between Christ's first and second comings. What then of the mark this beast gives? Do we need to be concerned about credit cards, driver's licenses, social security numbers, and the like which contain this number? Does it not make more sense to see that just as God has sealed his people as a sign of ownership, so the beast of the earth seals those who are his. Those who belong to the beast are "marked" by the fact that they live according to his values, standards, and principles. It's easy to tell them apart from those who belong to Christ and refuse to lead lives marked by the world's values or to affirm its principles. This is less a 666 tattoo, and more a telltale affirmation of what people really value and who they really follow.

The consequences for the people of God are obvious. To confess that Jesus is Lord and that Caesar is not is to find it oftentimes very difficult to buy and sell—that is, to carry on an interrupted life in the midst of a corrupt and anti-Christian world and culture. Manifestations of this kind of persecution were happening in first-century Rome for believers who refused to burn incense to Caesar. And in every generation since, the cost of following Jesus rather than the dragon and his minions has been documented by tears, blood, loss, privation, and even death.

During my life, 99% of the discussions I have heard about the mark of the beast have given rise to speculation, doubt, and fear. But consider what next fills John's vision after God has given him insight into the diabolical trinity. "Then I looked, and there before me was the Lamb, standing on Mount Zion, and with him 144,000 who had his name and his father's name written on their

---

2. Philip Edgcumbe Hughes, *The Book of the Revelation* (Grand Rapids, MI: Eerdmans, 1990), 154.

foreheads" (14:1). Rather than being left to dread Satan and to fear his ways, John is led to worship God and delight in *his* ways!

Jesus stands on Mount Zion, the place of redemption. He is the victor over the dragon, the sea beast, and the earth beast. With him are all of his people, sharing in his victory. They are signed, sealed, and delivered safely to the Father by the triumphant Lamb. What's more, above both the sea and the earth with their beastly threats comes a better vision that overrules them.

John sees three angels flying in midair. These angels represent a God-centered view of the main issues of life between the two comings of Christ. As it turns out, spiritual warfare is not a story of cosmic conflict between good and evil, battling it out in the heavenlies and on the earth. More accurately, spiritual warfare is about the advancement of the gospel among the nations of the world in the midst of real, but ultimately futile, opposition.

The first angel proclaims the gospel to the whole earth, speaking of grace and impending judgment. Let God's people be encouraged: until the last hour, the gospel will be preached among the nations! The second angel warns that "Babylon" will fall. All godless systems and philosophies of the world are doomed. God's truth and kingdom will prevail over everything the dragon and his allies can muster. The third angel highlights the eternal consequences of every person's worship. To worship the beast is to be guaranteed eternal torment. To die in the Lord is to be guaranteed eternal rest.

This is the urgency of the gospel we proclaim, the main issue in life and in death. To whom have you given your worship? As Bruce Metzger has put it, "Men and women are so constituted as to worship some absolute power, and if they do not worship the true and real Power behind the universe, they will construct a god for themselves and give allegiance to that. In the last analysis, it is always a choice between the power that operates through inflicting suffering, that is, the power of the beast, and the power that operates through accepting suffering, namely, the power of the Lamb."[3] There's simply no such thing as a non-worshiper.

DISCUSSION *10 minute*

The article mentioned that the world usually makes it costly to follow Jesus. What has following Jesus cost you?

If the way of worldly power is to inflict suffering while the way of Christian power is to accept suffering, how should that affect the way you tell the gospel?

---

3. Bruce M. Metzger, *Breaking the Code* (Nashville: Abingdon Press, 1993), 77.

10

EXERCISE

THREATENED BY THE BEASTS

15 MINUTES

Our passage in Revelation explains that we are threatened by both the INSTITUTIONS of this world and its IDEOLOGIES. Work through this exercise on your own. Note some ways you have felt these threats, and also how it encourages you to see that the gospel advances in spite of them. When the group is ready, you'll share and discuss some of your responses.

Threatening Institutions. Where have you felt pressure to put allegiance to governments or other powerful institutions ahead of your allegiance to Jesus? Or where have you seen these institutions oppose God and his kingdom?

> ❐ **Nation.** I have felt pressure to be a "good citizen" of my nation first and a Christian only secondly at best, and only in ways that don't counter national expectations.

> ❐ **Powerful people.** I have seen those with power use it for their own gain instead of using it to help those in need or to pursue justice.

❐ **Politics.** I have felt the sway of a political party or voting bloc pressuring me to adjust my faith to conform to its political agenda.

❐ **Governments.** I know of governments who support other religions while actively opposing Christianity and the church.

❐ **Courts.** I can identify laws in my own country or other countries that discriminate against kingdom values and those who would follow Christ faithfully.

❐ **Workplace.** I have felt pressure to be a "good worker" in my company or to spout the company line, following Christ only so far as it does not "get in the way of my work," make anyone uncomfortable, or challenge company values.

❐ **Family.** I have felt pressure to conform to family expectations, and to place loyalty to my family ahead of loyalty to Christ and his expectations.

❐ **Community.** I have felt pressure to affirm the values and priorities of the people around me, and to avoid professing faith in Christ, affirming what he values, or pursuing his priorities.

❐ **Other:** _____.

Threatening Ideologies. Where have you felt the attack of the world's "wisdom" and ideologies, discrediting your faith and deceiving the world's people about what it means to follow Christ?

❐ **Mocking.** I get attacked by claims that my faith is obsolete, backward, or only for people who aren't intelligent.

❐ **Accusations.** I get told that my faith in Christ is hurtful to others.

❐ **Rejection.** I get shunned or labeled a problem by claims that my faith sets me against my family, nation, employer, etc.

❏ **Distain.** I get denounced as standing in the way of the world's view of progress and human flourishing.

❏ **Persecution.** I, or others I know, have been arrested, threatened, or harmed physically because of Christian beliefs.

❏ **Lies.** I get belittled or harmed by untrue claims about who Jesus is, what the Bible says, and what Christians believe or practice.

❏ **Other:** _____.

The Gospel Advances. How are you encouraged by the vision of the three angels: that despite these threatening institutions and ideologies, the gospel is still proclaimed throughout the earth and still advances, and will win in the end?

❏ **Comfort.** I realize I am not alone, nor am I crazy for feeling threatened. The Bible anticipates these threats, and believers in most times and places have experienced them.

❏ **Courage.** I stand firm because these threats will not last forever. No kingdom but Christ's, and no creed but the gospel, is truly timeless.

❏ **Mission.** I am eager to join the gospel's advance. I have a vision for how it can make inroads in the very nations, workplaces, families, and communities that seem so threatening. I want to reach people in those places.

❏ **Witness.** I am eager to tell and to show how the gospel is more glorious than the false ideas that attack it.

❏ **Kingdom Prayer.** I have a growing awareness of how God's people are being persecuted around the world and am eager to stand with them in prayer.

❏ **Renewal.** I am personally encouraged by the gospel in the midst of these struggles. In my need for comfort, I am drawn closer to Jesus—and so, the gospel advances *in me*!

☐ **Other:** _____.

When the group is ready, share and explain some of your responses. How does the pressure from the "beasts" make you feel? Are you frustrated, angry, afraid, or something else?

Where do you feel yourself giving in and *not* being persecuted by the beast, accepting his "mark" instead? Can you check *this* box?

☐ I have stood up for Christ and refused to "wear the mark of the beast"—that is, refused to do something immoral or dismissive of Jesus—knowing it would cause me to miss out on something the world offers.

How would you like to have a bigger vision for the advancing gospel in the midst of this world of beasts?

WRAP-UP AND PRAYER *10 minutes*

As part of your prayer time together, you might pray for protection from the world's influences, for courage to remain faithful to Christ, and for the spread of the gospel.

ASSIGNMENT: The next lesson will cover Revelation 14:14 through the end of chapter 18. You will only be reading chapter 18 together during group time, so please <u>prepare for the next lesson in advance by reading</u> **Revelation 14:14–17:18** <u>on your own before your group meets</u>.

The theme of that section of Scripture is God's judgment finally coming upon the beast and those who worship the beast. Judgment and the wrath of God are necessary topics in this world where the beasts we've just seen still roam with much freedom. Chapters 15 and 16 describe seven bowls of God's wrath that will remind you of the seven trumpets of partial judgment we've already studied. Chapter 17 and 18 describe the defeat of a great persecutor of God's people, pictured as a prostitute named Babylon the Great. Believers in John's time might have seen the prostitute as a reference to the empire of Rome, the city on "seven hills" (17:9) that persecuted them, but you will also be able to see parallels to persecutors that exist today.

11

JESUS TRIUMPHS
OVER EVIL

BIG IDEA

Jesus will triumph over evil and pour out his wrath on evildoers who reject him. This truth is sometimes hard, but ultimately help-ful to God's people.

BIBLE CONVERSATION *20 MINUTES*

In your on-your-own reading of Revelation, the vision of the dragon and his beasts continued with images of God's final judg-ment poured out on the earth and on those who worship the beast. Chapter 17 introduced an enemy of the Lamb, an adulter-ous prostitute labeled Babylon the Great. She too was brought to utter ruin and shame. The text calls her "the great city that rules over the kings of the earth" (17:18). Believers in John's day would recognize that city as Rome, whose emperors ruthlessly perse-cuted them. But believers in every age have faced persecution from wicked rulers and cities, and will until Christ accomplishes the final destruction this passage describes.

With this in mind, now read **Revelation 18**, which is about the aftermath of the prostitute Babylon's destruction. Have a few readers take turns reading aloud, and then discuss the questions below:

How does heaven's commentary on Babylon's destruction differ from what the people of earth say? Describe the difference in both what they talk about and their attitude.

What bothers you, or impresses you, about the attitude of either the angels or the people of the earth? Explain.

How is the boulder tossed into the sea an accurate image of God's final judgment? What feelings does it arouse in you?

****

Now read the article, "Jesus Wins!" Take turns reading it aloud, switching readers at each paragraph break.

JESUS WINS!

5 MINUTES

The first cliché I remember hearing associated with Revelation was, "I read the end of the book and we win!" To a competition-minded, sports-loving young Christian of the late '60s, that sounded great. It reminded me of the feeling I got when it was time to play neighborhood baseball or football and I knew Jimmy Richards was on my team. Jimmy exceled in any sport he played. If Jimmy was on your team, you could be assured of winning, period.

I guess I thought of Jesus as a big Jimmy Richards and the Christian life as the greatest of all sporting contests. Because Jesus was on *my* team, I knew I was destined to win! Such was the me-centered view of the life of faith I had in those early years. But as I have continued to study God's Word, my perspective has changed radically. I have discovered that the Son does not revolve around me, I revolve around the Son! Each of us matters, but only Jesus is the point.

Perhaps a better way of summarizing the later chapters of Revelation would be, "I read the end of the book and Jesus wins! He triumphs over all things, including us!" He has triumphed over my sin, death, rebellion, and unbelief. Jesus isn't merely on our team to help us win in life. We are engrafted into his heart and made partakers of his very inheritance! And as we have seen throughout the book of Revelation, God's love is meant to be the means by which we are freed from a life of self-preoccupation, unto a life in which we extend his grace to fellow sinners and reveal his glory among the nations.

This is the perspective meant to be cultivated by the sobering section of Revelation to which we now come. The concept of the wrath of God is, understandably, a very difficult one for many of us to accept, both intellectually and emotionally. This is especially the case in a human-centered culture in which the prevailing view of God asks how he might be useful to us. Without a vision of God's holiness, we tend to think of him as a benign grandfather who is somewhat under obligation to do us good—more of a sugar daddy than *Abba*, Father. And we tend to think of ourselves not as sinners who desperately fall short of the glory of God and whose only appropriate cry to God is for mercy, but as victims who need to be understood, "gotten," and coddled.

Like John, we need to see God's holiness and glory afresh. Only then will his grace and mercy move us to humility and gratitude for so great a salvation. And only then will we be able to understand and accept the revelation of his wrath that is to come in full upon the world. God's wrath is not the irrational rage of an irritated pagan deity. Rather, it is his righteous indignation toward all evil and his resolute action in punishing it. It is precisely because God is love that he brings judgment upon everything that contradicts his beauty and perfection. One day we will understand this—when we behold God's unfiltered glory.

In Revelation 15 and 16, we witnessed the coming judgment upon those who have tried to make life work apart from God's saving grace and without bowing the knee to the true King. In chapters 17 and 18, we are given a vision of the end of the evil characters that have perpetuated Satan's foolish attempt to usurp God's glory. "The beast and the ten horns you saw will hate the prostitute" (17:16). Satan's kingdom will ultimately be divided against itself and fall! God will cause evil to collapse beneath the tonnage of its own rancor and rebellion.

What comfort this must have been to Christians living under the persecution of mad Roman emperors like Nero. The first-century historian Tacitus reports that Nero falsely accused Christians of setting fires, but then "a vast multitude was convicted on charges not so much of arson as of hatred for the human race. And they were not only put to death, but put to death with insult. They were either clothed in the skins of wild beasts and then exposed in the arena to the attacks of half-famished dogs, or else dipped in tar and put on crosses to be set on fire, and when the daylight failed, to be burned as lights by night" (Annals XV, 44).

This explains the exuberance when a most glorious angel whose splendor lights the whole earth arrives in John's vision to announce with a shout: "Fallen! Fallen is Babylon the Great!" The day of God's vengeance has come. Defeated evil will become eradicated evil. She will be paid back double for her crimes! Hope is stirred within the church, while lament is generated among the kings, merchants, ship owners, and sailors who have profited from the prostitute. Sadly, these are not tears of repentance. These are selfish tears over the loss of worldly position, power, and possessions. With the downfall of the prostitute also comes the judgment of all who have loved her ways.

A mighty angel throws a huge boulder into the sea to symbolize the violence with which Babylon will be thrown down, once and for all. Life will never be the same in Vanity Fair. Her pleasures and magic spells were for a season, but now the season is up. Evil will cease to exist. Hallelujah!

DISCUSSION *10 minutes*

How does it make a difference for you to think of the Christian life as one where God wins rather than one where you win? (You might consider its effect on your worship, how you treat others, or your witness about Jesus.)

How does your awareness of God's holiness need to grow? How might your thinking about evil and judgment be different if it did?

Lesson

11

EXERCISE

WHY GOD REVEALS HIS WRATH

15 MINUTES

Because our anger is corrupted by self-centeredness, it can be hard for us to see the value of reading four chapters in the Bible that celebrate wrath. So for this exercise, consider some of the reasons why God wants you to see a vision of his wrath and judgment.[4] On your own, read through the reasons below and note those that most speak to you. When the group is ready, you'll share some of your thoughts.

WHY GOD SHOWS US IMAGES OF HIS WRATH

1. **So we will see the seriousness and ugliness of our sin.** We are always prone to take our sin too lightly, imagine it isn't so hideous, or make excuses for it. The jaw-dropping images of wrath in Revelation are a sobering reminder to flee from sin daily, to learn to hate it, and to be humble before our grace-giving God.

2. **To give us awe for God's holiness.** Our view of God will be stunted, and we will take serving him too casually, unless

4. These reasons are based in part on those given by Arthur W. Pink, *Studies in the Scriptures 1930–31* (Lafayette, IN: Sovereign Grace, 2001) 5:96.

we get a soul-shaking look at his holiness. Revelation shows how God's perfections and love are flat-out incompatible with the least bit of evil. God is *that* good and pure!

3. **To deepen our gratitude for salvation.** We need to see how dire our predicament was and what we deserve. As we read the vivid accounts of God's wrath in Revelation, we realize that they symbolically depict everything Jesus suffered when he took that wrath in our place. What a loving Savior we have!

4. **So we can rest in the vengeance of God.** When evil is done against us, we need not spend our lives fuming or getting even. We can be assured that God's justice will be more complete than ours ever might be—and carried out in perfect righteousness. Revelation allows us, despite our anger at so much, to live as people of love.

5. **To make us urgent about missions.** Perhaps we need to have our comfortable view of things shaken. The world is in dire need of the message of salvation and the love of Christ. We need to leave our comforts behind and take the gospel into the world before the fearful judgments of Revelation come to pass.

When the group is ready, discuss. Which reasons best help you understand why God would tell us about his wrath, and why? How might you still need to ponder further?

There is also an emotional side to the Bible's teaching about God's wrath. You may be feeling some of the following:

☐ <u>Grief</u> over people you know who seem to be under God's judgment

☐ <u>Anger</u> with God over his apparent failure to punish evil or to save certain people

☐ <u>Fear</u> about the eternal destiny of people you love

☐ <u>Doubt or frustration</u> at not being able to fully reconcile God's love with his wrath

It helps to remember that the Savior who judges the nations in Revelation is the same Jesus we know through the Gospels. He has shown us *his* emotional life. For example, we have seen him weep over the people of Jerusalem who refused to recognize him (Luke 19:41–44) and drip sweat like blood in anticipation of suffering God's wrath in our place (Luke 22:44). Because we know him, we know that his anger is not moody, mean-spirited, or self-serving like ours. Unlike us, "with righteousness he will judge the needy, with justice he will give decisions for the poor of the earth" (Isaiah 11:4).

How does the fact that the judge is Jesus help you work through your emotions about judgment?

WRAP-UP AND PRAYER *10 minutes*

It may feel odd, but one of the best ways to respond to the topic of God's wrath is to pray to him about it. Pray that he would give you the understanding he wants you to have. Especially if you are struggling to believe that God is fully good, he invites you to take that struggle to him and work through it with him. Don't hide your struggle from the one who is able to help you in it.

Lesson

12

JESUS AWAITS A WEDDING

BIG IDEA

Jesus is eager to celebrate being with his people forever once he defeats our great enemy.

BIBLE CONVERSATION *20 MINUTES*

Following Jesus's final triumph over evil, Revelation 19 gives a vision of two feasts. The first is the "wedding supper of the Lamb" where Jesus is forever united with his bride, the church of believers. In stark contrast, the second is the "great supper of God" where birds are invited to gorge themselves of the bodies of his defeated enemies.

Now have a few readers take turns reading **Revelation 19** aloud. Then discuss the questions below.

Describe the atmosphere surrounding the wedding supper of the Lamb. How does it differ from popular depictions of a believer's arrival in heaven or first time meeting Jesus?

The vision of the heavenly warrior gives Jesus four different names: (1) Faithful and True, (2) Word of God, (3) King of Kings and Lord of Lords, and (4) a name no one knows but he himself. How do these names fit what happens in the vision? Which name do you most appreciate, and why?

****

Now take turns reading the article aloud, switching readers at the paragraph breaks, and then discuss the questions that follow.

A WEDDING LIKE NONE OTHER

5 MINUTES

One of my earliest and most naïve prayers as a young Christian was, "Heavenly Father, please do not send Jesus back to earth before I have a chance to get married." The thought of going to heaven without ever experiencing "spousehood" was not really all that exciting. In fact, I had an underlying fear that heaven might not be quite as heavenly if I entered as a single man. Where such a notion came from, I cannot tell you!

Well, God over-answered that prayer. He brought an amazing woman named Darlene into my life, whom I've had the privilege to call my wife for forty-eight years! She has loved me well and has been a primary means of God's grace to me. Among the many lessons God has taught me through marriage to a wonderful woman, none is more important than the call to constantly ponder Jesus's love for his bride, the church—of which, I must consistently remind myself, I am a part.

Only the love of Jesus can fill us up. As much as Darlene has been an astounding blessing to me, there is no spouse (or any human being, or group of them) in the world who can possibly meet the deepest longings of the soul. Jesus is the spouse we've always

115

wanted. Only Jesus, our perfect and passionate Bridegroom, can satisfy the craving for ultimate intimacy that rages within us. I have found that the more I am preoccupied with the inexhaustible love of Christ, the more I move toward my wife to give rather than to demand.

Another eternally important lesson the Father has been teaching me as a married man is that joy and freedom come from meditating on the future wedding of the Lamb. This vision is calculated to thrill and encourage all Christians who live between the two comings of Christ. Just as the warfare intensifies in the closing visions of Revelation, so also the theme of Jesus's love for his bride grows in its glory and grandeur!

Jesus is coming for his bride, his beloved whom he will forever have and hold. Let this vision go deep into your heart, for I have discovered no aspect of the gospel with greater power to bring forth hope, focus, and persevering love in the midst of the worst assaults the dragon and his allies afflict during our journey toward our true and lasting home. We are not just going to heaven. We're heading for our wedding celebration and marriage to the Lamb of God, Jesus.

Revelation 19 opens with an awesome worship celebration in response to the destruction of the great prostitute. Before the wedding of the Lamb is announced, we find rejoicing over God's judgment upon this false lover. Throughout the Scriptures, God speaks of his people's compromise with the culture's "gods" as adultery. When we sin, it is not just against God's law, but more emphatically against his love. God has a holy jealousy for our affection, and the destruction of Babylon says as much about God's love for his people as it does about his hatred of evil.

"Hallelujah!" roars the multitude in heaven. This is the only place in the New Testament where we find this praise word. How appropriate that it would be reserved to underscore God's intimate and involved love for his bride. Jesus is getting ready to receive his beloved for whom he died. We are a people dressed in pure linen, the garment of his perfect righteousness and of the righteous acts of service we offer him for so great and grace-full a salvation. What a marriage banquet this is going to be!

To fully appreciate this exquisite passage, it helps to have a basic understanding of the marriage customs of the Jewish culture in which Jesus was raised. First, there was a legally binding betrothal. Paul uses this image to describe our relationship with Jesus this side of his second coming: "I promised you to one husband, to Christ, so that I might present you as a pure virgin to him" (2 Corinthians 11:2). Then came the interval, during which the groom would pay a dowry to the father of the bride.

As the interval drew to a close, preparation for the procession would begin. The bride would adorn herself. And the groom, with his good friends singing and carrying torches, would make his way to the home of his beloved. After receiving his bride, the procession would return to his home where a great feast, including the wedding supper, would last from seven to fourteen days. Very few celebrations could compare with the joy and happiness of a wedding feast in that culture.

Just think of it: our wedding feast with Jesus is not going to last a mere seven or fourteen days. It is going to last throughout eternity, rejoicing with the love of our life and with the whole bride redeemed from every people group in history! At this point I am reminded of how Paul wrote, "Eye has not seen, nor ear heard, nor have entered into the heart of man the things which God has prepared for those who love Him" (1 Corinthians 2:9 NKJV). Surely, he must have been thinking about our marriage to the Lamb.

John is so overwhelmed by the glory of it all that he simply *has* to worship, and he starts to worship the angel, who corrects him. Oh, that such awe would overtake us as well, as the hope of our wonderful future captures our imaginations and our hearts! We are the bride of Jesus, his betrothed. He cannot love us more! He will not love us less! We are in the wonderful interval period. There is no dowry left to be paid. The procession is not far away.

DISCUSSION *10 minutes*

Compare the popular idea that heaven is merely a reward for good people with the Bible's view that it is a wedding Jesus eagerly awaits. How does it affect the way you feel about the life to come, and how you prepare for that life?

How does being filled by the love of Christ help you give love to others rather than demand love from them? Explain with an example, if you can.

Ezek 37, 39
biord prophecy

Lesson

EXERCISE

FIGHTING FOR JESUS OR WITH JESUS

15 MINUTES

Before Jesus takes his bride into eternity, he thoroughly destroys all of her adversaries. The vision of the rider whose robe says "King of Kings and Lord of Lords" gives us a second look at the fire-eyed, sword-wielding Savior we met in Revelation 1. This time, he is in action. He who first came into the world to suffer returns as a warrior-judge, leading the armies of heaven in conquest of the beast and the false prophet.

Beyond informing us about the second coming, this vision also teaches us how to think about spiritual warfare. Any concept of spiritual warfare which does not begin with a vision of Jesus as the divine warrior is simply insufficient. It is he who leads us against his own enemies. We are not fighting *for* him, to impress him, but *with* him!

On your own, read through the differences between fighting *for* Jesus and fighting *with* him. Note some that are meaningful to you—perhaps areas for growth, or ways you recognize yourself. When the group is ready, you'll discuss what you noted.

119

Fighting FOR Jesus (to impress him)	Fighting WITH Jesus (by faith)
I feel I must defeat sin in my life so I can show God some progress.	Jesus is defeating sin in my life. He leads me into that battle, where I join the fight at his side.
I don't pray much, not feeling the need, nor do I think I've really earned the right for my prayers to be heard and answered in love.	I pray often. How else could I resist Satan's temptations, deflect his accusations, and overcome fear?
My efforts to obey God and help his kingdom advance are based on my willpower and "giftedness."	My efforts are grounded in the sharp sword of Jesus's Word. I read it, listen to it preached, believe its promises, and let it guide me. It has power in me.
My default mind-set is insecurity. I know I need to be more faithful to Jesus, and that he must be displeased with my efforts.	My foundation is eternal security. I am Jesus's forever-loved bride. My efforts to be more faithful to him flow out of his perfect faithfulness to me.
To me, humility means I admit I am often unfaithful, and so my confidence is low. Just call my name Wishy-Washy.	Humility means my confidence is not in myself but in Jesus. My confidence is high because *his* name is Faithful and True.
I find it's best for my reputation that I avoid serving outside my areas of expertise, and it's best for my self-esteem if I skip fighting sin that's proven too hard to overcome.	Because of my Christ-esteem, I realize that when I am weak, he is strong. He rides out and slashes all enemies, not just a select few.

When the group is ready, share some of your thoughts. Which items feel familiar when you think of your life? Which do you want Jesus, the fearsome rider, to strike down in you? Which do you most want him to build up?

WRAP-UP AND PRAYER *10 minutes*

You can take a key step in fighting *with* Jesus merely by praying right now. Most of us are too slow to pray, so make it one of your requests that your Father would transform you into a person who prays often.

Lesson

13

JESUS GIVES A NEW HOME

BIG IDEA

The final judgment of all people who have ever lived will usher in not just a new life, but a wonderfully new world, for those whose names are known by Jesus.

BIBLE CONVERSATION *20 MINUTES*

The first part of Revelation 20 describes a period of a thousand years, commonly referred to as the millennium. Believers who share a conviction that the Bible is true and trustworthy have nevertheless disagreed over how to interpret this passage and, therefore, how to think about the millennium. If you are interested in a summary of the major views, you may consult the appendix in the back of this book. But for this lesson, it is necessary only to know that all these views see the millennium as a period of partial victory before the end-times judgment of the dead and the appearance of a new heaven and a new earth, which are this lesson's focus.

Have some readers take turns reading **Revelation 20:1–21:8** aloud. Then discuss the questions below:

In chapter 20, what aspects of God's power over Satan do you find especially encouraging, and why?

Most scenes in Revelation feature great throngs of people, but the judgment scene mentions each person being judged individually. How does that strike you?

From the description of the new heaven and new earth, what do you think you will find most different and captivating about living there?

****

Next, read the following article aloud, taking turns by paragraph.

ARTICLE

A NEW HEAVEN AND A NEW EARTH

5 MINUTES

That our Lord finishes his written Word with a magnificent vision of a new heaven and a new earth is exhilarating, and worth pondering. Last words are lasting words. Final images are formative images. God wants our hearts to be consumed with a vision of our forever. But it's not merely the thought of heaven that matters. *What* we think of this glorious state of existence is even more important. It's critical to how we invest our lives until Jesus returns.

Much of my early imaging of the afterlife came from Saturday morning cartoons, bad hymns, and television commercials. I remember thinking that everybody who goes to heaven probably becomes an angel, or morphs into cute, cherub-like creatures. The atmosphere of heaven always seemed misty and surreal. The music was an annoying blend of soprano choirs accompanied by harpists and organ music. God, if represented at all, spoke with a deep, synthesized voice, more robotic than inviting. Why I ever wanted to go to such a place, I do not know. Maybe because it seemed better than the alternative!

But at age eleven, thinking about life after death took on a new importance. I came home from school one day to the tragic news that my mother had been killed in an automobile accident. All of a sudden, angels and harps and clouds meant nothing to me. Not being a Christian at the time, I had no spiritual resources to draw upon and no real assurance about anything.

Older, well-meaning friends tried to comfort me with statements like, "Your mom is in a better place." Sentimental images of my mother "having fun" were used in an attempt to deaden the pain of her being ripped from my everyday life. It wasn't until seven years later, when I became a Christian, that I began to understand the living hope our Father has in store for his children. My joy was intensified to realize that though I wasn't a Christian when my mom died, she was.

What, then, does God want us to know about the life after this one? Much as the Bible begins with the story of God's first creation, it finishes with the hope of God's new creation. For much of my life, I must confess, I assumed heaven existed somewhere "up there." If you go to heaven you have to leave earth.

Most certainly, Christians who die before the return of Jesus Christ are taken immediately into the conscience presence of God, where they enjoy rich community with those who have preceded them. Yet as wonderful as their experience is now, it is not complete. Of the current population of heaven, only Jesus has his resurrected body. Believers have yet to enter into the full inheritance that will be the eternal portion of the people of God after Jesus Christ returns to the earth to consummate history. There is a deep longing in our hearts for this day, one no other circumstances can satisfy.

And it is not just us who await the full inheritance of heaven: "The creation waits in eager expectation for the children of God to be revealed. For the creation was subjected to frustration, not by its own choice, but by the will of the one who subjected it, in hope that the creation itself will be liberated from its bondage to decay and brought into the glorious freedom of the children of God" (Romans 8:19–21). The atoning death of the Lamb of God is so powerful and magnificent that it will also usher in a remade world no longer under sin's curse!

Do not gloss over the grand affirmations at the start of chapter 21, or miss their glorious implications. Jesus is making all things new; he's not making all new things. We live in a story of redemption, not replacement. The great hope we share is not to get out of this mess but for Jesus to put all things right—or as J.R.R. Tolkien suggested near the end of his Lord of the Rings trilogy, to make everything sad become untrue. This bears enormous implications for our understanding of how we are to live between the comings of Jesus. All of history is tied to our Father's commitment to redeem an every-nation bride for Jesus and to, eventually, make all things new through Jesus. We are to live on mission with a view of the day when there will be no more death, mourning, crying, or pain—the day when God's glory will fill the earth "as the waters cover the sea" (Habakkuk 2:14).

Defeated evil will become eradicated evil. This is what John means when he says there will no longer be a sea in the new heaven and new earth. He's not describing a new-creation world without beaches! In Revelation, the sea is the place of chaos from which the dastardly beasts emerge. Their defeat was secured by Jesus's cross. Their eternal demise will happen at his return.

When we read the Bible as one big story, unfolding from Genesis through Revelation by the plotline of creation, fall, redemption, and restoration, we realize that Eden was a glorious preview of coming attractions. The end of God's story is much more glorious than its beginning.

This means it is more accurate to say heaven is going to come to us than to say we are going to heaven. Our eternal celebration will not take place somewhere up in the clouds, but right here in God's renewed world. I love the Swiss Alps and have sometimes commented that if the new creation is as beautiful as Switzerland, I would be a satisfied man. But I expect that when the present creation is liberated from its bondage, I am going to have to repent of being far too easily satisfied. There is no way our pre-glorified senses can begin to imagine the full glory of the new creation to be revealed.

But as satisfying as that beauty will be, the main truth God shows us about heaven in these final chapters of Revelation is its *relational* beauty. What makes heaven most heavenly will be the way our Father loves us—his entire, every-nation family. He has already perfectly reconciled himself to us, and us to him, through the death of Jesus. Nevertheless, there awaits the fulfillment of promises that have stood since Adam and Eve rebelled in the garden of Eden.

The theme of *Immanuel,* "God with us," by which God pledges to be our God and make us his children, runs throughout the Bible. Now John is told, "He will wipe every tear from their eyes." In Greek, this phrase means so much more than just the elimination of our tears. It highlights the redeeming of the pain behind the tears.

Lest these images be interpreted as the overstated projections of a wistful apostle in exile on Patmos, God puts his own pledge on the promises of paradise. "Write this down, for these words are trustworthy and true." It is impossible for our God to lie. There is nothing more to be done to secure this blessed state for God's people. Therefore, the great invitation once again goes out: "To the thirsty I will give water without cost from the spring of the water of life." The price has been paid. All we have to do is drink!

DISCUSSION *10 minutes*

What default views of heaven have gotten into you, and where have they come from? How might your views need to change or expand?

Consider the difference between longing for the comforts and *physical* beauty of heaven, and longing for the *relational* beauty of life with Jesus. What might that difference look like in your life?

Lesson

13

EXERCISE

FIVE WAYS JESUS SAVES

15 MINUTES

The vision of a new heaven and a new earth reminds us how far-ranging our salvation is. Jesus is saving us from sin in multiple ways that add blessing upon blessing. If we limit our view of salvation to only a few of those blessings, our joy and gratitude and the way we live for Jesus will suffer.

On your own, read the descriptions of five of the main ways Jesus saves his people from sin. For each, notice what happens if we (1) tend to forget or downplay that part of salvation or (2) tend to forget or downplay everything *but* that part of salvation. Ask yourself what your tendencies might be. When the group is ready, you'll discuss some of your findings.

Jesus saves me from THE GUILT OF SIN. The blood of the Lamb, shed on the cross, has paid for my guilt. Jesus took the punishment I deserve.	
When I forget or downplay being saved from guilt . . .	When I forget or downplay *everything but* being saved from guilt . . .
I live with insecurity, seldom enjoying God or feeling truly thankful, and instead wondering what he thinks of me.	I feel saved from hell, but there's little thrill. There's nothing glorious I'm saved *into*.

128

Jesus saves me from THE ALIENATION OF SIN. I am no longer an exile, but a child of the Father and a bride of the Lamb—loved, cared for, listened to, and given a home and inheritance.

When I forget or downplay being saved from alienation . . .	When I forget or downplay *everything but* being saved from alienation . . .
My life with God feels flat and lonely. It lacks joy, since I fail to love God himself.	My life is little more than a quest for a God-and-me, feel-good experience. I neglect the hard work of loving others.

Jesus saves me from THE POWER SIN HOLDS OVER MY LIFE. Satan is no longer my lord. With the Spirit's constant help, I have power to say no to Satan's temptations and fend off his accusations, and to adorn myself in holiness.

When I forget or downplay being saved from sin's power . . .	When I forget or downplay *everything but* being saved from sin's power . . .
I get lax about living as befits Jesus's bride. My witness, integrity, love, and confidence in Christ all suffer.	Following Christ feels like a constant slog as I struggle to be good without the comfort of God's forgiveness and eternal delight.

Jesus saves me from THE DEATH THAT SIN BRINGS. My name is in the book of life. My body will rise from the dead and live with God forever.

When I forget or downplay being saved from death . . .	When I forget or downplay *everything but* being saved from death . . .
I live for whatever I can get out of this life, protecting myself ahead of serving others.	I treat Jesus as little more than someone I can use to get into heaven.

Jesus saves me from THE EFFECTS OF SIN IN THIS WORLD. A new heaven and new earth is coming, free from mourning or crying or pain, and it will be my eternal home.

When I forget or downplay salvation from this world's troubles . . .	When I forget or downplay *everything but* salvation from this world's troubles . . .
My gospel witness lacks compassion or the sense that Jesus cares about evil and is committed to ending it.	My gospel witness is little more than social reform or do-gooding dressed up to look "Christian."

Now share some of your thoughts with the group. What are some of your tendencies to forget or downplay a part of the gospel? How would you like to grow?

What effect does your awareness of the full picture of salvation have on your commitment and confidence to go into the world to love others?

WRAP-UP AND PRAYER *10 minutes*

Be sure to pray for the growth you want in your awareness of how fully you are saved. Pray especially for specific ways your hope can be centered in the new heaven and new earth.

Lesson

14

COME TO JESUS'S GARDEN

BIG IDEA

History is moving toward a perfect conclusion that fulfills God's eternal plan for his people. He and we together say to the world, "Come!"

BIBLE CONVERSATION *20 MINUTES*

We come now to the final pages of the Bible, which in many ways parallel its opening pages found in the first few chapters of Genesis. What creation anticipated, the new creation completes. What sin destroyed, Jesus repairs. Have some participants take turns reading **Revelation 21:9–22:21** aloud. Then discuss the questions below:

What objects or events from the early pages of the Bible do you notice being restored, reversed, or improved on in this passage?

REVELATION: HOPE IN THE DARKNESS

Note some of the perfections of the new city described here. Which perfection do you find most striking, and why?

What are some of the final few things God says to us in the closing paragraphs of the Bible, and why do you think he says those particular things?

✳✳✳✳

Now take turns reading the article aloud, switching readers with each paragraph. Then discuss the questions that follow.

132 *Lesson 14: Come to Jesus's Garden*

Lesson

PERFECTION AND FULFILLMENT

5 MINUTES

This lesson's section of Scripture challenges another of my cherished but wrong notions of heaven. For years, I thought we Christians would be spending eternity walking on streets of gold, having gone through the pearly white gates into the eternal city whose cubical walls are made of all kinds of precious jewels. And if we were really fortunate, our mansion would be next door to Jesus. But now I find out that we, the wife of Jesus, are the city—a people enjoying perfect relationships and perfect everything else.

How are we to understand the vision of the holy bride-city coming down from heaven? Once again, we need to realize that John's numbers and images are well-chosen symbols to meditate upon rather than literal statistics to mechanically draw. It seems that through this picture of the wife who is the new Jerusalem, God is most zealous for us to celebrate at least two great truths.

First, this is a promise and picture of the perfected bride of Christ, the glorified church. How stunning and encouraging such an image must have been for the seven fledgling churches spread around Asia Minor! We may feel small and despised today. But one day we will glow not with the beauty of Cinderella but with the very glory of God. The bride-city is twelve thousand stadia in length, breadth, and height—the dimensions of a cube. Why a perfect cube? In the temple Solomon built in Jerusalem, the Most Holy Place measured twenty cubits by twenty cubits by twenty cubits (see 1 Kings 6:20). This was the center place of God's presence among his covenant people. Now, life in the new heaven and new earth will be like one giant Most Holy Place on steroids—the presence of God unfiltered, permeating all things. God who began a good work in us will bring it to perfect completion on the day of Jesus's return.

Second, our Lord once again emphasizes the fulfilled relationship with his people in this magnificent description of the Jerusalem. John notes, "I did not see a temple in the city, because the Lord God Almighty and the Lamb are its temple" (21:22). As in the garden of Eden, so in the new heaven and new earth there is no need for a physical gathering space to worship the triune God. The entire family of God lives all of life before his unhidden face and grace-full gaze. God's glory enlightens the whole realm through the Lamb! The gates are never closed because fellowship and communion with God will never cease. Everyone whose name is written in the Lamb's book of life is always welcome.

The angel next shows John the river of life. Ezekiel and Zechariah longed for the day when living waters would flow from Jerusalem in the messianic age. Philip Hughes comments, "The river with its water of life symbolizes the inexhaustible grace of God."[5] This is the joy-producing "river whose streams make glad the city of God, the holy place where the Most High dwells" (Psalm 46:4).

Straddling the river on both sides is a massive tree, "the tree of life, bearing twelve crops of fruit, yielding its fruit every month. And the leaves of the tree are for the healing of the nations" (22:2). It takes no biblical giant to recognize the connection between this garden and the garden of Eden. That which was forfeited by sin

---

5. Hughes, *The Book of Revelation*, 232.

in the first garden is now restored beyond measure in the garden of the new Jerusalem.

The tree of life, from which Adam and Eve were forbidden to eat after they sinned, now becomes the year-round symbol of the welcoming and nourishing heart of the throne of God and of the Lamb. The leaves of the great tree remind us that even as the gospel is now the greatest healing force in the history of mankind, so in heaven the healing of the nations will come to completion. The substantive healing we can know in this life will give way to the fullness of his peace in eternity.

"No longer will there be any curse." The curse Adam and Eve brought upon themselves and the whole creation is now lifted, due entirely to the work of the Lamb who "redeemed us from the curse of the law by becoming a curse for us" (Galatians 3:13). Every semblance of sin in us, and around us, will be gone forever.

"They will see his face, and his name will be on their foreheads" (Revelation 22:4). For Moses to have seen the face of God would have meant death, but for us in heaven it will mean a level of intimacy, joy, and fellowship with our Lord that we can only imagine. There will be no one unknown or unloved in our eternal state of blessedness. Even now, through the riches of God's grace, we are totally known and completely loved.

How shall we be occupied in this perfected state? According to the Scriptures, we will serve him and reign for ever and ever. The entirety of eternity can simply be called "worship service." For the first time since the fall, all of life will be lived as an unbroken worship service. In heaven we will be fully and finally freed to obey the greatest of all commandments: to love the Lord our God with everything that we have and are. Free at last, free at last, thank God Almighty, we will be free at last!

DISCUSSION *10 minutes*

The article suggests the blessings of the new life might be summed up as *freedom*. What do you think of that? Do any other words come to mind?

In Revelation 22:17, both the Spirit (God) and the bride (the church) issue the invitation to come, and then those who hear pass along the invitation as well. What about this final vision might you want to tell to others, and what is your role in the echoing call to the world, "Come!"?

Lesson

14

EXERCISE

THE COLORS OF JESUS

15 MINUTES

Let's finish our study of Revelation the same way it began, by looking at Jesus. Revelation has given us a series of colorful pictures by which we can know him and his work of salvation. So for this exercise, think in terms of some of the colors we've seen connected to the Savior. Read through the descriptions on your own. Consider how your view of Jesus has grown by studying Revelation, and how you would like it to grow still more. You'll share some of your results once the group is ready.

Jesus in WHITE. He is the Lord who rides out in righteousness, purity, and truth, on a white horse. He puts his people and his bride in pure white too. He is the Savior who makes you holy and delights in your purity.

    ❑ My appreciation for this aspect of Jesus has grown.

    ❑ I especially want to grow more in appreciating Jesus for this.

Jesus in RED. He is the rider whose robe is dipped in blood. He executes God's wrath, but does so as the slain Lamb who has willingly taken God's wrath for his people. And so, he has freed you from the full curse of your sins, by his blood.

❏ My appreciation for this aspect of Jesus has grown.

❏ I especially want to grow more in appreciating Jesus for this.

Jesus in GOLD. On his head are many crowns, and his city is made of pure gold. He has been awarded dominion over everything in heaven and on earth. His great pleasure is to bring you into his city and share the riches of this inheritance with you.

❏ My appreciation for this aspect of Jesus has grown.

❏ I especially want to grow more in appreciating Jesus for this.

Jesus wielding BLACK. He rules the nations with an iron scepter. He will strike down every enemy that oppresses his people. Your persecutors will not be able to stand when he appears in his glory.

❏ My appreciation for this aspect of Jesus has grown.

❏ I especially want to grow more in appreciating Jesus for this.

Jesus among the GREEN. He brings his people into a new garden, with a tree for life and leaves for healing. He is the Redeemer not just of you, but of the world where you will live without death or mourning or crying or pain.

❏ My appreciation for this aspect of Jesus has grown.

❏ I especially want to grow more in appreciating Jesus for this.

Jesus of EVERY COLOR. His city's foundations are decorated with every kind of colorful stone—twelve precious gems, representing the full number of his dearly-loved people (see Exodus

28:15–21). He is gathering for himself worshipers out of every nation to enjoy his glory forever, and you are included. As you answer his call to come and drink, by drawing near to him daily, you also go out and say to others, "Come!"

❒ My appreciation for this aspect of Jesus has grown.

❒ I especially want to grow more in appreciating Jesus for this.

Share and explain some of your choices. What have you seen in Revelation that has enhanced your appreciation for Jesus? How do you hope to grow more?

WRAP-UP AND PRAYER *10 minutes*

Pray together that your time in God's Word, increasing your foundation in the gospel, will continue even once this study has ended. Perhaps you want to make plans for more study together.

CLOSING NOTE FROM THE AUTHOR

It has been nearly twenty-five years since I first taught all the way through the book of Revelation at the Art House, culminating in writing my first book, *Unveiled Hope*. Revelation continues to be my favorite of all the sixty-six books in the Bible. Why? Because it assumes everything that is written in the other sixty-five books is God's Word, and because it most expressly reveals Jesus to be the central figure and only true hero in the entire history of redemption and restoration.

Indeed, the gospel is the good news of Jesus, by Jesus. Our understanding of the Bible is only as good as our grasp of everything it says about the person and work of Jesus. The gospel is a glorious person first, and trustworthy propositions only secondly. It is some*one* before it is some*thing*. So my question as I anticipated writing an epilogue to this study guide was, "How can I faithfully and creatively represent the awesome ending of Revelation?" How can I do justice to this magnificent book which shows how Jesus is God's emphatic "Yes!" to everything our Father has promised in his Word? Then it occurred to me that Revelation 22:6–21 is how God, the primary author and architect of the Bible, chose to conclude the entire Bible!

Last words are lasting words. What does our Father want to impress upon our hearts?

> **"These words are trustworthy and true" (v. 6).** What we have seen and heard and found written here finds its source in God. We can stake our lives on it and fuel our hope with it.

"Do not seal up the words of the prophesy of this scroll, because the time is near" (v. 10). We must continue to exalt Jesus, invite others to trust him as their Savior, and proclaim his kingdom through deeds of mercy and justice. This is our calling until the day Jesus returns to finish making all things new. Jesus's return is "near" in terms of implications and proximity. We are to live certain of his return and all the astonishing benefits of his second coming. And we are to live with great anticipation of that day, which could be within our lifetime.

"Look, I am coming soon!" (v. 12). Jesus will return, not a day too soon for his patient mercy nor a day too late to keep his sure promises. All of history, as we know it, is leading unalterably to the justice of the final judgment and the jubilation of the gathered, every-nation bride of Jesus.

"Blessed are those who wash their robes" (v. 14). Those who may go through the gates into the city and who have access to the tree of life are those who have "washed their robes and made them white in the blood of the Lamb" (7:14)—not those who have tried to earn life within the city by their own good works and self-righteousness. The dividing line in eternity is always drawn between those who receive the death they have merited by their sin and those who escape death by trusting in the merit of Jesus Christ won upon his cross. There is nothing more important to understand in the whole Bible. The only basis upon which we can have any confidence to stand before God on the day of judgment is to have put our trust exclusively and completely in the finished work of Jesus Christ. There is no other hope so precious and so sure. Jesus isn't just our comprehensive forgiveness; he is also our perfect righteousness.

"The Spirit and the bride say, 'Come!'" (v. 17). The gospel of Jesus Christ is not just theological language to be understood; it is the good news to be believed, received, and shared. In the Bible, sound theology and worshipful doxology go hand in hand, leading to missional living and loving. The lyric and music of the gospel fuel the dance of the gospel, in which we love our neighbors and run with the gospel to the nations. Are you absolutely certain you have responded to this, the greatest of all invitations? Is the music of the good news still filling the chambers of your heart? Are you dancing the dance of God's great welcome and his every-nation, whole-cosmos salvation?

"The grace of the Lord Jesus be with God's people" (v. 21). Linger and marinate in this incredible reality. This is the last verse in the entire Bible, not just the last verse in Revelation. At the end of God's 66-book, 1169-chapter, 40-author revelation to us, his last word is the grace of the Lord Jesus Christ. What does God most want us to get deep into the core of our whole being? The unsearchable, inexhaustible, irrepressible riches of his grace for us in Jesus Christ. In Revelation, we have witnessed God's saving grace for all who receive forgiveness in the Lamb, his sustaining grace for his persecuted people, his sovereign grace over every crises and crucible of history, and his sufficient grace extended to his children called to live and to love faithfully until Jesus returns. How shall we respond to such a promise and benediction? May we affirm from our hearts the final "Amen" with which the Bible closes: Yes, Lord, your grace is sufficient for all things, in all places, all the time. Hallelujah, what a Savior! Hallelujah, what a salvation! Even so, Lord Jesus, come quickly.

LEADER'S NOTES

These notes provide some thoughts and background information that relate to the study's discussion questions, especially the Bible conversation sections. The discussion leader should read these notes before the study begins. Sometimes, the leader may want to refer the group to a point found here.

However, it is important that you NOT treat these notes as a way to look up the "right answer." In most cases, the best answers will be those the group discovers *on its own* through reading and thinking about the Bible passages. You will lose the value of looking closely at what the Bible says, and taking time to think about it, if you are too quick to turn to these notes.

Also remember that this study guide's articles consist mostly of condensed excerpts from the author's contributions to a longer book. For still more background and insight into Revelation, you may wish to consult that entire work. It is available for purchase as an ebook at the New Growth Press website.

LESSON 1: A VISION OF JESUS

It is stunning that a Savior so magnificent and fearsome would also be so approachable and quick to show kindness. He comes immediately to comfort John and puts his hand on him—a gesture of friendship, support, and commissioning. Jesus is breathtaking and even alarming, but he is those things *for us*, his people. He stands among his churches, and he reaches out tenderly to his apostle and friend. The entire scene is meant to offer us untold encouragement.

Your group may have more questions about apocalyptic literature and its symbolism. Be aware that both vague and familiar symbols fill apocalyptic literature. They are similar to our political cartoons in which certain images are readily identifiable. For example, in our day the eagle stands for the United States. In the first century, the sea monster stood as the great enemy of God, Satan. The drama between God and Satan, the evil age and the age to come, are played out in fanciful and spectacular imagery. In the end, God always triumphs. Evil is destroyed.

Although Revelation is called an *apokalypsis*, there are some major differences with other apocalyptic literature. Apocalyptic writing usually features a hero from the past giving his vision of a victory that will come in the future. But John is a pastor in the present, and he is writing not his own vision but the very "word of God" (1:2). John also bids us look not just to the future but also to the past in which the Lamb of God has already triumphed! The great battle has been won at Calvary, and the mop-up operation is underway! For John, prophesy is both a foretelling and a forth-telling. Yes, we look to the future for the full manifestation of the triumph of King Jesus. But we also live in the present with encouragement, hope, power, and purpose! Clearly, Revelation bears the marks of apocalyptic literature, but it is primarily written to call us to live to the glory of God, right here and now, with hearts filled with his peace. John is writing to encourage, not to confound. "Grace and peace," not perplexity and puzzle, should come from studying the last book of the Bible.

Does the symbolism mean we are not to interpret Revelation literally? The answer depends on what we mean by literal interpretation. To literally interpret any portion of the Scriptures, we must be careful to identify the literary genre of the text. The Bible contains many rich expressions of language and writing styles. To "rightly divide the word of truth," we must learn the appropriate rules for recognizing, reading, and interpreting each of these. Especially when reading image-filled and predictive parts of the Bible, we should be wary of hasty conclusions. Apocalyptic writing is full of symbolism, and prophesy is best interpreted by its own fulfillment! Enough is made patently clear in the Bible to keep us busy until God makes the less clear certain one day. Perhaps the best way to respond to the text of Revelation is the way John responded to his vision of the exalted Jesus—prostrate on our faces before the Lord it so clearly reveals. Such reverence, awe, and brokenness are becoming those who ponder what is taught in Revelation or, for that matter, in any of the Scriptures. Until "we shall know fully," may our textual and theological confidence be adorned with appropriate humility!

LESSON 2: JESUS'S LOVE FOR HIS CHURCH

We are given sparse information about the churches Jesus selected to receive his letters, only enough to know that Jesus sees what is happening with his people and cares deeply about it. It is not necessary to research the historical background of each city in order to understand Jesus's messages and the points he makes to each city. Rather, we should notice that his words are both specific to the struggles of each church (Jesus knows his people intimately!) and together make up a full summary of his instruction for all churches. Most likely, seven churches are chosen because that is a number of completeness. These are Jesus's words for all his people.

Jesus is direct in his letters. He doesn't soften things when he rebukes his people, as if the best protection against getting discouraged were to soft-pedal the seriousness of sin. Rather, he gives a stronger protection from discouragement: himself and his promises! Each letter opens with a reminder of who he is and closes with a promise for those who remain faithful. *This* is our encouragement when confronted with sin, either the sin in us or the sin in the world around us. We must look to Jesus and believe the promises of the gospel. Note that in Revelation these gospel truths especially include promises for the future:

- Those who are faithful will eat from the tree of life in paradise (Ephesus).
- Those who are faithful will not be hurt by the second death, the final judgment mentioned in 20:4–6 (Smyrna).

- Those who are faithful will eat with Jesus and be known by name (Pergamum).
- Those who are faithful receive the morning star, Christ himself (Thyatira).
- Those who are faithful will be acknowledged before the Father and his angels (Sardis).
- Those who are faithful will belong to God, bearing his name forever (Philadelphia).
- Those who are faithful will sit with Jesus on his throne (Laodicea).

These assurances help us stay faithful, especially in hard times. Hard times are normal, and even healthy for Christ's church. They direct us to our Savior and his promises. They may feel like poverty, but actually they are richness. Nothing is more precious than Jesus, and to be directed to his promises is pure gold.

LESSON 3: JESUS'S WORK OF REVIVAL

The three churches in chapter 3 have maladies which tend to occur together. They are dead and asleep, perhaps complacent about the opportunities God has set before them, and lukewarm about their faith. This is an all-too-common plight, especially in churches that start to feel they have experienced "success" or have entered a time of relative ease. Those successes and comforts become the treasures we seek, and we start to forget that closeness with God is the treasure we really need. When the fire for a closeness with God has turned lukewarm, deadness and sleepiness soon follow, and excitement for Jesus's mission and the opportunities he offers will grow cold.

The antidote is the same for each malady: we must strengthen what remains (v. 2) by holding on to Jesus's promises (v. 11) as we draw near to him. He invites us to answer his knock and eat with him (v. 20). We do this by approaching him regularly in prayer and in worship, and by reading and hearing his Word, which sets before us the luster of the gospel: We are forgiven by his sacrifice of love! We are redeemed from evil and emptiness by his precious blood! We are freely given a share of his Father and his glorious inheritance, and a role in his great mission!

As we are broken afresh by his love in the gospel, we receive true gold in the place of fool's gold. We gratefully put on the white garments of imputed righteousness in the place of garments which don't really cover our nakedness. We apply the salve of his grace that we might see what is true. Jesus calls us to love him with an undivided heart, with passion, above all else.

LESSON 4: JESUS OPENS HEAVEN'S DOOR

Many popular depictions of heaven feature a place marked by general emptiness and only one or two colors (white clouds and golden streets, perhaps). But the depiction in Revelation is one of fullness, including every possible color and creature. It is not a place where the rest of creation is forgotten and absent, but rather a place where all of creation is present and celebrated—and is celebrating its Maker. This should help us see that our God is not boring, but rather endlessly fascinating. He is not aloof from his world, but rather is involved and reigning. Life with him is not an escape from the world as much as it is an entry into the fullness and perfections of him and his creation. Worship of him is not monotonous and detached; it is a part of the splendor and variety of his whole creation.

God is not tame nor quiet. The sound associated with him is thunder—and, of course, worship. And worship is not limited to contemplative harp music, but is an eruption of boisterous praise. Heaven is not primarily about soothing, man-directed sounds designed to quiet our souls. Rather, it is about sounds directed not at us but at God. The sounds of heaven make our souls come alive because those sounds are all about the worship of the holy Lord Almighty. The primary sound of heaven is worshipful voices, importantly including human voices. We have been created to have a central role in this vivid scene that stands above the whole creation. Popular culture sometimes treats heaven as a place of whispers, perhaps so as not to disturb the sound of the harps. But it turns out that we and our well-heard voices have a key role in heaven's majesty.

The content of the worship in Revelation 4 confirms some of what we see suggested in the imagery: Our God is holy, almighty, and eternal. He is worthy to receive glory and honor and power. He is the creator and sustainer of all things, in control of his whole creation. He is the origin, source, architect, designer, builder, essence, reason, and end of *all* things. To see him upon his throne is to be humbled and gladdened, for our God has no equals or rivals. He will never be threatened, overthrown, or impeached.

Your group may be interested in more of the meanings behind the images in this chapter. We should hold our interpretations loosely and humbly, for some uncertainty is part of the nature of this type of revelation where we look into the hidden things of God that we may not fully know. But these are some of the possible meanings that fit the rest of Scripture:

- The rainbow is not only over all the earth, but also is a sign of God's mercy and covenantal faithfulness. Perhaps we are encouraged to think of the all-encompassing mercies of God shown in everything he does. From his throne flows a reign of mercy and faithfulness.

- The twenty-four elders probably represent the totality of redeemed mankind from both the Old and New Covenant, symbolized by the twelve patriarchs of Israel and the twelve apostles of Jesus. Their white garments represent the imputed righteousness of the Lord Jesus given to all who receive the grace of God in the gospel. The gold crowns signify both our calling to reign with him as a kingdom of priests and the rewards for faithful service which Jesus promises to his people.

- The lightning and thunder remind us of Mt. Sinai and other times when God spoke and acted in nature. The atmosphere of heaven is decorated with elements calculated to help us think of the awesome power and majesty of God.

- The four eye-encrusted living creatures are mentioned fourteen times in Revelation. It would seem that this quartet is meant to represent either all of animate creation or perhaps the order of angels known in the Bible as cherubim (see Ezekiel 10:20–22, for example). Both Ezekiel 1 and Isaiah 6 describe visions of angelic creatures which include their having six wings. The number four should make us think of the four quarters of the earth, the four winds, or the four compass points. Their many eyes seem to imply constant awareness and vigilance. Whatever kind of creatures they represent, they show us God's watchfulness over all he has made.

LESSON 5: JESUS RECEIVES WORSHIP

Genesis 49:9–10 is important for understanding how Jesus is the Lion of Judah. It is an early messianic prophesy, telling us that the earthly Israelite kings were only placeholders while God's people—and, indeed, the whole universe—waited for the one to whom the scepter truly belongs. This fits the despair seen in the opening verses of Revelation 5, as prospect after prospect fails to be the Messiah. And it underscores the joy when he finally appears, and the still greater joy that will be ours when he finishes his conquest. The fact that such a great Savior does this by humbling himself, suffering, and dying for our sin is perhaps the most poignant twist in Scripture's entire grand story. It reveals glories of Jesus that have an unsearchable depth. We can peer into them in wonder, knowing we still can't see the bottom.

The gospel as presented in Revelation's new song emphasizes both the sacrifice of Jesus on the cross and the end result for which Jesus went to the cross.

- "You were slain." Jesus's sacrifice is the zenith and purest expression of his costly and unconditional love for sinners.

- "With your blood you purchased for God persons from every tribe and language and people and nation." Jesus did not merely make redemption possible. He has actually secured the salvation of many from every people group.

- "You have made them to be a kingdom of priests to serve our God, and they will reign on the earth." Through Jesus, our lives have meaning, not just in eternity, but also in every community on earth where we might take the gospel.

This vision of the end result of Jesus's death and resurrection, and of the Great Commission that followed and is also a part of the gospel, should encourage us in our work for his kingdom. The people God reaches through us, and the communities we serve, have a future of untold glory brought about through this mission.

BIBLE CONVERSATION: Why is it hard to be humble and forgiving when we worship? One answer is found in the article's observation that we have begun to worship the worship experience rather than Jesus. When we come for the experience, we will often be disappointed. When that worship experience matters more to us than Jesus himself, it becomes an idol, and it is not surprising that we get annoyed when that idol fails to deliver what we selfishly demand from it. But when we come to worship Christ rather than our experience, we arrive humble and can set aside our worship preferences.

LESSON 6: JESUS BRINGS PURPOSE TO OUR SUFFERING

When we resist puzzling too much over the precise imagery, the descriptions in chapter 6 of life in a fallen world actually look familiar and fit common observations of what is wrong in the world. There is war and violence. There is economic maneuvering that takes advantage of workers and is greedy for their wages. And there is death by all manner of means, causing too large a fraction of the world's people to suffer an early demise.

However, this is not the end God has planned for his world. History is heading inexorably toward the great day of the Lord, when the nations of the world will be judged. The most important question on that day—and this day and any day—is "Who can withstand it?" (6:17). Who will be able to stand up to God's judgment? Each of us will either receive the love of the Lamb or the wrath of the Lamb. We can humble ourselves and receive the full and free benefits of Jesus's death on the cross for our sins, or we will despise his love and suffer the eternal implications and just consequences of our sins.

The cries of those who have rejected the Lamb do not reflect true repentance come too late, but rather the fear that comes from seeing Jesus when they know they are not humble before him. They are still intent on self-preservation, having never stooped to accept Christ's salvation. In contrast, Jesus's people are sealed and secure *in him*. They too cry out, but it is to proclaim his sufficiency on their behalf: "Salvation belongs to our God" (7:10). For them, service is a joy (7:15), and personal comfort from their God is their greatest reward (7:17).

For both groups of people, earthly distinctions cease to matter compared to the key question, "Are you sealed in Christ?" Kings and slaves alike who have rejected Christ call on the mountains to cover them, while believers from all nations and tribes stand together before the throne of the Lamb. Perhaps the number 144,000 is meant to suggest the twelve patriarchs of Israel times the twelve apostles of Jesus times one thousand (a number representing magnitude). This is a major theme of Revelation: God is indeed faithful to the covenant he made with Abraham. He has secured the salvation of his people not just from ethnic Israel but also from all the tribes of spiritual Israel (see Galatians 3:28–29; 6:16; Hebrews 12:22–24). What an international group, reflecting the magnitude of God's grace!

NOTE: Especially as you move into this section of Revelation, your group may want to understand that there are four main schools of thought held by Bible-affirming scholars when it comes to interpreting Revelation's end-times visions:

- The <u>preterist</u> view holds that Revelation is written in veiled language that's almost exclusively about events in John's own time, emphasizing that its symbols are to be understood in light of the Roman persecution of Christians and that empire's eventual destruction.

- The <u>futurist</u> view sees Revelation primarily as a book of prophecies concerning events yet to come, especially events that immediately precede the second coming of Christ.

- The <u>historicist</u> school sees in the text a charting of the complete history of the church between the two comings of Christ.

- The <u>idealist</u> school teaches that Revelation contains both concerns for first-century Christians and prophecies of the distant future, and so it consists of principles applicable for Christians in every generation.

It is important to realize that each of these four positions is championed by scholars who have high regard for the Scriptures, and who believe that the Bible is without error in all that it teaches. This study's position is that it is not necessary to embrace one of these schools of interpretation to the exclusion of the other three. We can gain valuable insights from all of them. Let us seek to maintain teachable and discerning hearts, and to hold our convictions on these matters lightly and humbly. Biblical prophecy sometimes has one immediate application for God's people who first hear it and also a richer meaning that becomes clear as his redemptive plan unfolds. Our study will be most interested in Revelation's message for us today as believers who are part of God's multi-generational family but live between Christ's two comings.

NOTE: Point out to the group the assignment for next time to read Revelation 8 and 9 before the group meets.

LESSON 7: THE LAST CHANCE TO BELIEVE IN JESUS

NOTE TO THE LEADER: This lesson covers chapters 8 through 10 of Revelation. Since this is too much to read during group time, you will be reading only chapter 10 as a group. Participants should read chapters 8 and 9 on their own before the group meets. You may want to remind them of this a few days before you meet.

Whether the angel in the vision stands for Jesus, or for evangelists, or is just an angel, it seems clear that the task of delivering God's word comes with beauty, awe, and power—and with great urgency. Yet, there is a paradox: the imposing angel holds a tiny scroll. The presentation of the gospel may seem simple to us, and the message itself not lofty or sophisticated (see 1 Corinthians 2:1–5)—like a little scroll held out in the hand. But the feet of those who bring good news are beautiful (Isaiah 52:7), and the expansion of God's word into the whole world is an event of momentous importance, described by Jesus as part of the gospel itself (see Luke 24:45–48). Like the angel pictured in Revelation, this work of mission connects heaven with every part of the earth, and has a staggering glory. The message may be unpretentious, but it arrives with a roar.

The gospel brings much joy, but in this world we often taste some sorrow and concern along with the pleasure. The gospel offers a stark contrast between salvation in Christ and judgment by Christ. This means that the urgency of saving sinners is as much a motivation to tell the gospel as is the joy of proclaiming the love of God. And the state of the world and its people, which are under God's curse due to sin (see Genesis 3:16–19), is a constant bitterness even as we realize that God is working through this curse to sweetly call people to himself. Even the Christian life is both sweetness and bitterness. We enjoy the untold sweetness of being God's loved and forgiven children, but our calling in Christ is to deny ourselves and lay down our lives for others, and to suffer persecution as our Savior did. In particular, the work of mission is full of paradoxes, just as this passage presents an impressive angel with an unimpressive scroll: Salvation comes through death and sacrifice. Wisdom is found in the foolishness of the cross. God's strength is seen in our weakness. We decrease so that Christ will increase. God's kingdom is breaking in with glory, yet remains hidden. And the path to sweet victory passes through bitterness.

DISCUSSION: It's important for us to see that God's partial judgment in these last days is a judgment that is still calling all people to repentance, and so it is full of compassion. Much like we speak of "tough love," God is showing kindness when he gets the attention of unbelievers through difficult events in the world and in their lives. When he does so, he makes clear the seriousness of sin and its horrendous effects on them and on those around them. He causes them to see their need for him. He teaches them to long for a day when evil is defeated and to seek the Savior who will bring about that day. And he provides the kind of world where we, his people, can wade into trouble spots to demonstrate the compassion of God to those who are suffering. All of this is part of his call to repent and believe the gospel. In Ezekiel 33:11, God says, "I take no pleasure in the death of the wicked, but rather that they turn from their ways and live." Likewise, we should not delight in death, even when it comes to the wicked, but rather should mourn with those who mourn and quickly fill our role in God's plan—responding in ways that show his compassion.

LESSON 8: WITNESSING FOR JESUS

The ministry of the two witnesses seems powerful enough at first. They clearly have God on their side. Yet they meet opposition and are killed. Their apparent defeat marks not just an end to their lives, but a great humiliation and disgrace. It is hard to see how things could get worse. But neither death nor humiliation is their final end, for their Lord is the Lord of life. God takes them through death into resurrection. The end result is that (1) they receive the public approval of God and (2) many who had not believed give glory to God. The witnesses' lives were hard, but their vindication was glorious and their impact was huge.

This is a common life-pattern for any of us who profess Christ with true boldness. Opposition will arise. God's enemies will seek to harm, disgrace, and humiliate us. But our patterns of dying—giving up security, comfort, self-interest, possessions, and more—lead to ultimate vindication and resurrection. The impact of our witness may be hard to see in this lifetime, but it surely is great.

The proclamation that "the kingdom of the world has become the kingdom of our Lord and of his Messiah" is, in many ways, the crowning end goal of all human history. The gospel is about salvation from sin in Christ, and this is the final defeat of sin as Christ reclaims both his world and his people from evil. The many types of evil have been seen in the seven seals and the seven trumpets. Evil inherent in a fallen world will end: no more thorns, dangers, scarcities, natural disasters, or death. Evildoers in the world will be defeated: no more oppression, fighting, persecution, or gloating. And evil in us will be purged: no more selfishness, unbelief, or fear. Both we and the world will be as creation intended.

NOTE: If your group wonders about the measurement of the temple at the beginning of the chapter, the most important aspect to note about the vision may be that John is instructed also to measure the worshipers there. This measuring is similar to what Ezekiel was commissioned to do in Ezekiel 40–42, but in the New Testament we find that the temple of God actually becomes the people of God (see 1 Corinthians 3:16–17; Ephesians 2:19–22; 1 Peter 2:5). John's focus is on the temple made of living stones, the people of God from every race, tribe, tongue, and people group, who are becoming a dwelling place for the Lord by his Spirit. As Philip Hughes has commented, "The measuring commanded here is an indication to us of the ordered perfection of all that God purposes and performs, as the Creator and Restorer of the universe. Its measuring may be taken to mean that God is in control of all that happens to his servants, they are well-known in number and name to God."[6]

EXERCISE: There are many reasons why it matters that Jesus led the way in a life of dying and resurrection, and that he died for us first before calling us to die for him. Here are a few of them:

- It makes our calling to die a duty of love rather than a harsh duty.
- It gives us the gratitude we need to be humble.
- It fills us with confidence that such a life is possible and will end in victory, and that God supports us in it.
- It shows us that the way of cross-like sacrifice is full of nobility and true glory.
- It gives us the comfort of knowing that although our attempts to love others will reveal much sin in us, we are loved and forgiven by God.
- It assures us of God's perfect love and care as we live sacrificially. "He who did not spare his own Son, but gave him up for us all—how will he not also, along with him, graciously give us all things?" (Romans 8:32).
- It gives us an unshakable hope in hard times that "God has raised us up with Christ and seated us with him in the heavenly realms" (Ephesians 2:6).

LESSON 9: JESUS DEFEATS THE DEVIL

Those familiar with Matthew's account, in particular, of Jesus's birth will see parallels with the description in Revelation 12. The dragon's attempt to destroy the child the moment he is born reminds us of King Herod, and God's protection reminds us of the flight to Egypt. Indeed, much of Jesus's life on earth was spent keeping a step ahead of those who wished to kill him until he

6. Hughes, *The Book of Revelation*, 120.

willingly gave up his life, was raised from the dead, and then was caught up to heaven. The vision in Revelation goes through these events quickly, but does allude in verse 11 to the way Christ's victory came through suffering and death.

Those familiar with the rest of Scripture may also see allusions to the larger redemptive story. Revelation 12 connects Israel's escape from Egypt and perseverance in the wilderness to the redemptive story by picturing the woman (God's people) as fleeing to the wilderness and being nourished there by God. And in verse 5 it connects the kingly rule of David and his descendants to the redemptive story by quoting Psalm 2:9, "You will break them with a rod of iron." That psalm is originally about the power given to Israel's king, but this passage in Revelation, along with 2:27 and 19:15, indicate it is also about King Jesus. Even the devil's appearance as a dragon should sound familiar. He appears as a serpent the first time we encounter him in the Bible in Genesis 3, and is reptilian again in Isaiah 27:1. His multiple heads and horns show his power. And the way he sweeps stars out of the sky may be a clue to the backstory behind him and his demons, which is mentioned in 2 Peter 2:4 and possibly alluded to in Isaiah 14:12–15, and has been imagined in many works of fiction.

One way the perspective in Revelation gives new insight is its emphasis on the battle between heavenly forces. Whether the war between Michael's angels and the dragon's angels is merely a colorful description of Jesus's victory by the cross and empty tomb, or represents an actual heavenly battle that took place at the same time or thereafter, the text highlights the *spiritual* aspect of Jesus's victory. He did not just save us from our sin; he also conquered powerful forces amassed against us.

Another important insight we can get from the heavenly perspective is the intensity of the devil's pursuit of us, God's people. There is no mistaking its serious nature. It is a very real and persistent threat, and this passage should serve as a warning for us to remain constantly aware of it. It is not clear whether the passage is saying that the devil is defeated twice and God's people pursued into the wilderness twice, or is merely telling about the same event in two different ways. Whichever it is, the key takeaway for us should be the twofold point that the devil is ultimately defeated but is still a dangerous threat for a limited time (symbolically, 1,260 days). This is a key reality that should inform how we live until Christ returns.

We can also gain some important tactical intelligence about our adversary. Satan is a cunning deceiver (v. 9) who wants us to believe his lies. He is an accuser (v. 10) who wants us to feel condemned despite the blood of Christ. He uses these lies and accusations that come from his mouth to try to sweep us away (v. 15). He is very angry, and operates out of spite and hatred. If he comes against us, it is not because he ultimately may be able to claim us but because he is resentful that he cannot.

For this reason, true believers should expect spiritual warfare and sharp attacks in this world. We also should be looking constantly to our Savior, who can bear us on eagles' wings to places of safety in this wilderness (see Exodus 19:4).

LESSON 10: JESUS AND HIS PERSECUTED PEOPLE

We do not need to look outside of our own time, either back to the Roman Empire or ahead to some future world power, to recognize the character and the tactics of the beasts. The character of the beasts is to blaspheme God, slander his name, and attempt to take for themselves the worship that is due him. Perhaps the sea beast's deceit is so presumptuous that it even counterfeits the death and resurrection of Jesus through its fatal wound that has been healed. The tactics of the beast are based on coercion and deception. By their apparent control of the commerce of the world and the ideas of the world, the beasts attempt to force the world's people into compliance—and they kill when they can't get their way. This stands in stark contrast to the tactics of the Lamb in chapter 14. Although he has the power to force all people to bow the knee before him, his method is to purchase and redeem his people through self-sacrifice and love, allowing himself to be killed. This makes the worship of Jesus so much better! It is not a coerced lie (14:5), but a beautiful roar of joy.

The appeal of this better, true worship is itself a great motivation to proclaim the gospel to the nations. The stark contrast between the fates of those who serve the beast and those who worship the Lamb is another. The fact that the gospel rings out above the entire earth and sea, with a message both far more beautiful and more powerful than the lies of the beast, ought to make us eager to join in its proclamation. Praise God that the gospel advances despite every scheme of the beast! God gives us this vision as a gift, that we might be filled with hope as we assume our role in his sovereign plans and purposes.

NOTE: Point out to the group the assignment for next time to read Revelation 14:14 through the end of chapter 17 before the group meets.

LESSON 11: JESUS TRIUMPHS OVER EVIL

NOTE TO THE LEADER: This lesson covers Revelation 14:14 through the end of chapter 18. Since this is too much to read during group time, you will be reading only chapter 18 as a group. Participants should read the earlier chapters on their own before the group meets. You may want to remind them of this a few days before you meet.

The heavenly voices are triumphant about Babylon's defeat. They especially celebrate the thoroughness of Christ's victory: the city is not only destroyed, but has fittingly become a place for demons and disgusting things, and it is destroyed never to rise again, so that no one will be led astray or slaughtered anymore. Heaven's exuberance over the city's fate, including the end to perfectly acceptable activities like music-making and marriage, may seem at first like gloating. But the final freedom of God's people has been a long time in coming, and ought to be celebrated. And the voices of heaven are supremely interested in the welfare of God's people. Even the city's seemingly benign features may not be allowed to entice those Jesus loves. His people must come out to the safety of their Savior, while Babylon receives a double portion from her own cup of crimes.

In contrast, the kings and merchants and captains from the earth mourn the loss of Babylon mostly out of self-interest. They see the victory God has won for his people, but they have little real regard for the welfare of God's people or anyone else. Thus, even the mourning for Babylon consists of selfishness that will soon disappear from the earth.

The boulder tossed into the sea brings to mind God's final instructions to the prophet Jeremiah when he spoke against the original Babylon, an Old Testament enemy of God's people: "When you finish reading this scroll, tie a stone to it and throw it into the Euphrates. Then say, 'So will Babylon sink to rise no more because of the disaster I will bring on her. And her people will fall'" (Jeremiah 51:63–64). Babylon's doom is a great plummeting, down to the depths of the sea, where it will never rise again and will be forgotten in the new joy of God's redeemed people.

LESSON 12: JESUS AWAITS A WEDDING

Many popular depictions of a believer's arrival in heaven feature a quiet, peaceful, or ethereal experience. Or perhaps believers are stopped at the pearly gates for a gut-wrenching moment of decision where St. Peter determines whether or not they will get in. The emphasis is entirely on the believer's fate and happiness. In contrast, the emphasis in Revelation 19 is on the exuberant joy of Jesus—and of all of heaven with him. The welcome is loud, even boisterous. The praise is overwhelming. There is a realization that the moment is not just about the salvation of individual believers, but about the long-awaited joy of Jesus as he brings his people home. Revelation 19 also contains no lingering emphasis on the believer's sins or "tsk, tsk" from St. Peter as he looks over the record and finds some concerns. The bride has been made perfectly pure by the sacrifice of Christ and the sanctifying work of the Spirit. She is celebrated, not tolerated, in heaven.

The names assigned to Jesus in this passage are rich in meaning. Among the truths they likely signify are the following:

- The name *Faithful and True* stands in contrast to Satan who is a liar and accuser, who will have all his schemes foiled, and who cannot be trusted to have our best interests in mind even when his temptations seem enticing. Jesus can be trusted to accomplish what he promises and to work all things together for our good. And *his* testimony before the Father, declaring that we are his beautiful bride, will topple the empty accusations of the dragon.

- In part, the name *Word of God* represents Jesus's power over all things to be the one to accomplish God's purposes. The same powerful word by which Jesus created the world (Genesis 1:3), maintains the world (Hebrews 1:3), quiets storms (Mark 4:39–41), heals the sick (Luke 7:6–8), and raises the dead (John 11:43) is now the word by which he slays all of his and our enemies.

- *King of kings and Lord of lords* shows the royalty and absolute rule of Jesus, and is appropriate for the rider who strikes down the forces of evil with ease. The quotation from Psalm 2:9, "He will rule them with an iron scepter," is recorded here for the third time in Revelation. The psalm celebrates how God brings down the puffed-up kings and other rulers of the earth who fail to bow before him.

- The name no one knows but he himself is fitting for the eternal Son of God. He is so far above us that there is a sense in which no name we might comprehend can do him justice or fully reveal his glory. At some point in our inquiries into the names of Jesus, we are wise simply to take to heart his words in Judges 13:18: "Why do you ask my name? It is beyond understanding."

LESSON 13: JESUS GIVES A NEW HOME

Sometimes lost in discussions about the millennium is the way Revelation 20 pictures God's absolute dominance over Satan. Whatever is meant by Satan's binding, he is totally at God's mercy. He is pictured as restrained by a giant chain in a bottomless, shut, and sealed pit—and it only takes a single angel to do it! He is made helpless to deceive the nations while those whose murders he orchestrated are brought back to life and honored. Even when he is released again, this is God's doing, his time is limited, and it all serves to set up a great victory for God and torment for Satan's allies.

The judgment scene before God's throne shows that God sees the hearts and actions of individuals, even to the extent that the details are pictured as written down next to each name. Each person, living or dead and important or plain, will be judged by their actions in life. It is sobering to realize that God knows us by name, including all we have done. But it is also comforting to those who realize they have been saved by Christ and have their names in the book of life. Back in 13:8, we were told that the book of life is the slain Lamb's book, planned from the creation of the world. This means our names are not there by our merit, but by Christ's atoning sacrifice and God's eternal plan. Our place in the new creation, where God knows our name, is secure—because it rests in him and not in us.

The new heaven and new earth we will inhabit is beautiful, not chiefly for the gold and precious stones that will be mentioned later in the chapter, but for the end of suffering and the comforts of God. He promises three blessings in 21:6–7. There will be free water for the thirsty, an inheritance for the victors, and himself as Father.

One more thing: those who love the ocean need not be troubled by the mention that there will no longer be any sea. The sea is a metaphor for chaos and evil. It would not be surprising to find the beauty of the beaches of the new earth far surpassing anything that we have known before!

LESSON 14: COME TO JESUS'S GARDEN

Participants who are familiar with the beginning of Genesis will see that the last few chapters of the Bible parallel the first few chapters in several ways:

- One Old Testament reference in this part of Revelation is the appearance of a city called Jerusalem, which John sees from a great and high mountain. Although worship on Mount Zion in Jerusalem was introduced later in the Old Testament, the description of the garden of Eden in Genesis suggests it too was located on a mountain, as a river flowed out of it (see also Ezekiel 28:13–14). In any case, mountains are associated in Scripture with worship and are places where God meets with his people. The New Jerusalem is a place of perfected worship and nearness to God—the fulfillment of what Eden began.

- The gold and gemstones mentioned in Revelation also call Eden to mind (see Genesis 2:12). Later in the Bible, gold adorns the tabernacle and temple where God is worshiped, and gemstones represent God's people when the high priest wears a gem-studded breastpiece to appear before God (Exodus 28:15–21, see also Zechariah 9:16).

- The tree of life first seen in the garden of Eden appears again in Revelation 22. There is no biblical report that Adam and Eve ever ate from that tree while in the garden (indeed, they were barred from the tree after they sinned), but in Revelation every resident of the New Jerusalem is invited to share from this tree. This communion with God is not merely a restoration of Eden, but the fulfillment of what Eden never turned out to be.

- The Bible begins with the creation of the heavens and the earth, and it ends with a new heaven and new earth. It begins with day and night, light and darkness, sun and moon, and it ends with a city that has no night nor any need for the sun and moon because the darkness is gone.

- The effects of sin and the fall are overturned too. The sin, curse, and death seen in Genesis 3 are eradicated at the end of Revelation. And in place of a guarded gate, no sinful person may enter is a city whose gates are never shut. The tree in the heavenly city will not usher in sin, but will bring healing to the whole earth.

The New Jerusalem is perfect in glory and brilliance. Its perfect dimensions suggest a perfect holiness. Its worship does not require a temple (which is merely a pattern of heavenly worship), but is perfected by the presence of God himself, the perfect temple. It features the sort of life we, who have only ever known imperfection, can hardly imagine: perfect purity, perfect happiness, perfect blessing, perfect service of God, and perfect intimacy with God.

The closing verses of the Bible give us several important truths that are good for believers in every age to keep in mind:

- Jesus is coming soon. We must live each day with this in mind. It is a way to keep our focus on the treasures of heaven rather than on earthly things, which are a constant temptation. And it is our great comfort when life in this world is hard. We must learn to make "Come, Lord Jesus" our daily prayer and cry.

- There is a stark contrast between those who believe the gospel and those who don't. We are either inside with Jesus or outside among those who love and practice evil. We must make our choice. It is *the* choice of our lives, the choice of eternity.

- God and his word are true. We can be comforted and have no doubts. And we must never imagine, as we are often inclined to do, that we can come up with some better or more palatable truth. There ultimately is no assurance in such self-made doctrine, only despair.

- The invitation of the gospel still rings out, and what a glorious call it is! Our chief duty is simply to know our own thirst and to come with gratitude to the Savior who provides the free gift of living water. As we drink deeply, we also go out to share the invitation with others. What joy!

- We are not to seal up the words of this book, because the time is near. While the opportunity remains, we are called upon to bear witness to the reality of heaven here on earth, inviting others to know Jesus as their Savior. Regardless of our calling, sphere of influence, or location, each of us has an important part to play in proclaiming God's kingdom through our words (evangelism) and deeds of mercy and justice.

- The grace of the Lord Jesus is with his people. We are not without a helper. We are not dependent on ourselves. We are people of Jesus and of untold grace.

APPENDIX: MILLENNIAL VIEWS

Revelation 20 tells of a thousand-year reign of Jesus, often called the millennium. Historically, debates about this period of time have caused separation between Christians. My main concern is for us to ponder the importance of being very careful not to be overly dogmatic about something we are given so little information about in the text of God's Word.

Yet, questions may be formulated in our hearts as we read this text: What is meant by the thousand-year period? When does the binding of Satan take place, and in what sense is he bound? What are the first and second resurrections? How does the millennium connect to the second coming of Jesus? These questions lead me to present a basic overview of the three main schools of millennial thought that have been developed by thinking Christians in the church. It is important to note that each of these schools of interpretation is represented by believers who affirm the absolute inspiration and authority of the Bible, our brothers and sisters who have lived and died for the glory of Jesus Christ.

PREMILLENNIALISM

This position is often born out of a belief that the book of Revelation should be interpreted as literally as possible: numbers and images are to be taken at face value unless a symbolic intent is clearly obvious. Premillennialists also stress the importance of accepting the sequence in which John received his visions as the sequence in which these events will happen in history. Thus, this school of interpretation maintains that the thousand years of John's vision is to be taken as an actual period in history of about a thousand years. Central to premillennialism is the conviction that Jesus Christ will return to earth in order to inaugurate this long season of peace and righteousness—thus the name *premillennialism*. Christ returns *before* the millennium.

There are variations, but most premillennialists believe there will be a first resurrection of Christians at the beginning of this era. A thousand years later, Satan will make a final attempt to deceive the nations, leading to a final showdown between his kingdom and the kingdom of God, and a second resurrection that takes place along with the final judgment.

We should all respect how committed the premillennialist is to the "plain sense of the text." The words of the Bible are to be taken seriously. Revelation should not become overly spiritualized or simply treated as a recording of John's mystical experiences. We should also appreciate the future orientation of this view. Premillennialists take the study of last things seriously. They celebrate a linear understanding of history that can get lost in the other positions.

POSTMILLENIALISM

This view maintains that John's vision of a thousand-year period refers to a growing state of peace, prosperity, and victory which the gospel will produce throughout the world before Jesus returns to the earth. So, Christ returns *after* the millennium. Those who hold to this school of interpretation emphasize the prophecies of the Old Testament, which speak of the advancement of the gospel throughout the world not just with respect to the conversion of many from every nation, but also with reference to the healing of the nations. They emphasize our calling as Christians to be involved in all areas of life and culture and to repent of the defeatism of much contemporary Christianity.

Many who have historically held to this position lived through great revivals and reformations in their lifetimes, leading them to believe that God will accomplish the same universally as a testimony to the power of the gospel and the glory of Jesus Christ. They invite us to study these revivals, that our hearts might be stirred with confident faith and expectancy.

We should all respect how the postmillennialist encourages us to believe that the gospel is much more than the means by which we can go to heaven one day. We should ponder the power of the gospel to affect all spheres of life: politics, education, economics, the arts, and society. The optimism of postmillennialists is a helpful corrective to hearts filled with more fear than faith when pondering the future.

AMILLENNIALISM

Amillennialism maintains that the thousand years are to taken symbolically, consistent with the use of numbers found throughout Revelation. There is no calendar-calculated thousand years. Rather, the millennium is the entire period of time between the first and second comings of Christ, who presently reigns from heaven with his saints. Jesus is acknowledged to be the King of kings and Lord of lords *now*, having ascended to the right hand of the Father.

Amillennialists emphasize the defeat of Satan won by Jesus upon his cross. The binding of the enemy refers to his no longer being allowed to keep the gospel hidden from the nations of the world. Heaven already is being filled up with men and women from every nation. The first resurrection, in this school of interpretation, refers to the resurrection of Jesus Christ in which all Christians share by virtue of their union with him. At the second resurrection at the end of history, all people will be raised from the dead to face the final judgment.

We should respect how amillennialism avoids the extremes of both faithless pessimism and exaggerated optimism by acknowledging how the Scriptures teach that the wheat and the tares will grow together until Jesus returns. The amillennialist invites us to consider the significance of the ascension and current reign of Jesus over all things, and to be driven by a vision of the cross— by which Satan has been defeated, and through which men and women from every people group in history are being redeemed.

*＊＊＊

How then are we to choose from among these options? To which does the whole of Scripture give the clearest witness? Once again, let me acknowledge that each of these positions has been championed by Christians who hold the Scriptures to be the inspired Word of God, inerrant and fully authoritative as the only rule of faith and life that God has given his people. Our decision is not a matter of choosing between conservative and liberal theological schools of biblical interpretation.

In my own journey in the land of millennial options, I feel no pressure to reach a dogmatic conclusion on "my position." The fact that men and women whom I love and respect in the Lord have settled into different millennial camps has actually brought freedom rather than confusion to my heart. And no matter which position proves to be true to the future unfolding of redemption, no Christian is going to be left out or disappointed. We are all going to fully enjoy everything won for us by our blessed Lord and Savior, no matter our position on the millennium!

I do describe myself as a "functional amil." After reading Revelation over and over, I have been led to embrace the essence of the amillennial position with certain qualifications. I appreciate very much the emphasis amillennialism places on the current exaltation and reign of Jesus Christ over all things. I am also drawn to the understanding that the binding of Satan primarily refers to the fruitful preaching of the gospel among the nations of the world.

But I also love the punctilious emphasis of the premillennialist on the imminent return of Jesus to the world. Many amillennialists simply do not seem to emphasize this anticipation, expectancy, and love for the appearing of our Lord as much as the Scriptures encourage. This is why I refer to myself as a "functional amil."

Amillennialism's "already and not yet" really makes a difference in the way I respond to the gospel. *Already* the kingdom of Jesus has broken into the world. He has poured forth his Spirit, and we are participating in the great harvest of men and women. But, *not yet* do we enjoy the fullness of the kingdom and of life as it will only be known when King Jesus returns. Therefore, my millennial view propels me to rest in his reign and, at the same time, long for his return.

mission
propelled by good news

At Serge we believe that mission begins through the gospel of Jesus Christ bringing God's grace into the lives of believers. This good news also sustains and empowers us to cross nations and cultures to bring the gospel of grace to those whom God is calling to himself.

As a cross-denominational, reformed sending agency with more than two hundred missionaries and twenty-five teams in five continents, we are always looking for people who are ready to take the next step in sharing Christ through:

- **Short-term Teams:** One- to two-week trips oriented around serving overseas ministries while equipping the local church for mission

- **Internships:** Eight-week to nine-month opportunities to learn about missions through serving with our overseas ministry teams

- **Apprenticeships:** Intensive twelve- to twenty-four-month training and ministry opportunities for those discerning their call to cross-cultural ministry

- **Career:** One- to five-year appointments designed to nurture you for a lifetime of ministry

spiritual
renewal
resources for you

Disciples who are motivated and empowered by grace to reach out to a broken world are handmade, not mass-produced. Serge intentionally grows disciples through curricula, discipleship experiences, and training programs.

Resources for Every Stage of Growth

Serge offers grace-based, gospel-centered studies for every stage of the Christian journey. Every level of our materials focuses on essential aspects of how the Spirit transforms and motivates us through the gospel of Jesus Christ.

- **101**: The Gospel-Centered Series
  Gospel-centered studies on Christian growth, community, work, parenting, and more

- **201**: The Gospel Transformation Series
  These studies go a step deeper into gospel transformation, involve homework and more in-depth Bible study

- **301**: The Sonship Course and Serge Individual Mentoring

Mentored Sonship

For more than twenty-five years Serge has been discipling ministry leaders around the world through our Sonship course to help them experience the freedom and joy of having the gospel transform every part of their lives. A personal discipler will help you apply what you are learning to the daily struggles and situations you face, as well as, model what a gospel-centered faith looks and feels like.

Discipler Training Course

Serge's Discipler Training Course helps you gain biblical understanding and practical wisdom you need to disciple others so they experience substantive, lasting growth in their lives. Available for on-site training or via distance learning, our training programs are ideal for ministry leaders, small group leaders or those seeking to grow in their ability to disciple effectively.

Serge Grace at the Fray   **Find more resources at serge.org**

newgrowthpress.com